RETHINKING LEADERSHIP

A Spirit-based Strategy for Global Influence and Moral Personal Development

Israel Chukwuka Okunwaye

On Rights and Permissions

Author/Publisher, ©Israel Chukwuka Okunwaye 2018.

For all correspondence, address to–
        27 Old Gloucester Street, London
        WC1N 3AX
        United Kingdom
        or, Email: write@israelokunwaye.com

Printed by *CreateSpace*, an Amazon.com Company. Available on Kindle and other retail outlets.

First published 2018

British Library Cataloguing in Publication Data
A catalogue record for this book is available from the British Library.

ISBN: 978-1-9164445-2-2
www.israelokunwaye.com
www.glyglobal.com

To my daughter, Gloria.

Preface:

People are rarely bothered about what name you ascribe to a food if it tastes good, it would seem to me. Give it a Turkish or Latin name– care less, if it is good and lawful, then bring it on. However, if the same meal has a name that ridicules a group, a word that stirs hate and associates with that which is foul and demeaning, or if the name suggests that certain religious rites have been applied to the preparation which conflicts with your principles, or that the meal itself is a gateway to some other occasion happening which you do not endorse– just then, eating a meal becomes suddenly difficult and not as easy as it appears. I gave this pointer to say, leadership goes beyond the act alone, though essential, to how and why one does the act or inspires others to. Leadership then enables the taking of responsibility, for oneself, and for others when opportune to. In this work, I set out core principles, and possibly not an exclusive list but rather indispensable, which I believe would help shape the minds of readers to contemplate thoughts on leadership they have not been privy to, or to further rehash values they may be familiar with but with more precise depth.

Rethinking Leadership: i – xciv

i. An elucidation of 'subliminal tactics' is about focusing on the core and allowing that to shape decisions and influence the right kind of productivity. I make a case that it is a tact you should have and desire. I give you four case studies. First, an illustration of a seed planted. The seed is covered by the soil, yet very important; even if not appearing. Visibility is not always significance. On the second level, is considering the biblical Joseph's illustration– he knew his potential was not dependent on being seen, so he honoured God whilst serving in Potiphar's house, amid the entrapments he found himself, so God honoured him openly, in high places [*Genesis 39*]. Also, more broadly a case of a secular company's value system, which often would shape its motto, vision and goals. It wouldn't be far-reaching if such values had some inherent connections to fulfilling a set of sound moral ethics deducible from biblical principles. This level of thinking which move from the surface to deeper streams of reason for perspectives adopted, would help understand what forms the motive for decisions and drive, either by a person or a group as an entity. On final example– the words of Jesus, which puts forward the thought that what comes out of a person is to be taken more seriously than what goes into them [*Mark 7:20*]; as words and concomitant actions would weigh more heavily than the food they consume in terms of what constitute who they are as a person. There are times we may need to be overt and outward looking in approach but remember what happens within is just as vital. A spirit-led leader should give thought to this and pray for divine help, as their internal thoughts would inevitably shape their words, whether twisted or not, and what actions they take on any matter. It's the summation of all that overtime that would define their personality and what they are known for. <u>A leader has to be aware of these levels of thought and seek to communicate consistently and incontrovertibly</u>

in whatever stream of engagement. So, you want to walk with God? You must be open to hear as He speaks. Is Christ asking you to receive water to drink from Him? Could it be He means more than water, and is calling you to something deeper [*John 4:1-42*]? Well, Christ may mean water, but understanding the context, and being tuned to spiritual frequency would enable you benefit from God's gift per time. This is so you don't settle for the elementary when God is calling you to the unseen. Well, be careful not to presume on the grace of God and mix the spiritual with the subconscious. Water may mean just water, if God wants it to so be, but another time could mean divine life— so be open to know, be careful to know, when God is requesting the seemingly ordinary from you, or when what He says becomes a metaphor for the divine. If God is in it neither is ordinary. The ordinary is the depth you are looking for if God is in it. Your depth becomes meaningless in the absence of God. The world cannot access the depth of God's spirit, because it is a deeper level of consciousness, which is a product of a supply of obedience and favour, not experience. Though we all can share a tribal language with perhaps a different level of understanding, of which God can delve in there too, to speak truth if it helps you, but don't mistake your human language, mnemonics, non-verbal communications and gestures, as spiritism– the Spirit's work is the birth processes of God orbiting divine graces. Whilst we pray to communicate the grace of God at all planes, it's the accompanying presence of God that surgically operates on conscience to heal and deliver, by God's divine word. To encounter a genuine richness of experience, God has to be centric to your search for meaning and every form of true and high grace. Haven said this, I must reiterate, the modern-day leader, in context of ever changing global technological and biological advancements, has to be mindful of his thought-process, and interact at varied levels of understanding, if sense has to be made of what becomes ethics. Taking responsibility for not just what is said but what comes across or what is understood. Usually the one who listens have to do that carefully, and with the right set of skills, in order to deduce rightly what is said. Nonetheless, the leader leads and so wants to ensure that the ideas trickle down properly and avoids chaos. So, where necessary he or she patiently recaps, emphasise, highlight keywords, breakdown notions, or illustrate. Except where being deliberately obtuse, which in itself admittedly is a skill. It's doing all possible to communicate to the proper audience, 'to stand–' doing all to ensure clarity is brought to a situation. It's different if those who hear choose not to hear or deliberately misinterpret– only have clean hands, showing you have done all possible to engage where you needed to, rather than being anxious over not maximising frivolities.

ii.   <u>It's not about competitor's competition, it is about purpose</u>. Focus on your task after discovering and defining it. The world's style of leadership is different from that of the Holy Spirit led leader–competition always exist in the world. It drains you to know those far or close with substantial connections may not just want to compete with you but eliminate any perceived threat to their chances, even when a rational mind knows this as unnecessary when unwarranted, especially when it is an opportunity open to all and enough for sustenance. Greed usually impedes rationality. Christ's way offers purpose! Why struggle with another if you knew your assignments were different, and that what you bring to the table is unique to you, as no one can deliver quite as you could, or would as occasion arise. Imagine the peace with yourself, knowing any attempt to clone your gift leaves whoever receives it less enriched than they could have been had they utilised the original. It's mainly not your loss. I wonder if any would prefer less than original if they could not afford the main deal, it appears so, however it impresses the need for the one with the gift to make sure they are accessible and functional for the right uses. In purpose there is meaning and life-long satisfaction. <u>By all means wish your competitors well but aim to leave your mark– 'to finish your own race.' People have a right to set their own goals, to compete for space, but I do not think they have a right to marginalise you</u> or to render you ineffective; this is why fairness and equity is necessary– again, if done according to these principles then you can accept the need to re-strategise to bring out the best in you. Think, 'how did I arrive at what I call my purpose? Do I just enjoy doing this or am I created for this?' Hopefully, both align. Sometimes God calls you for more. Ask Him prayerfully for direction. Your purpose is not competing with another but ensuring what God called you for is achieved. This is why you must wish everyone well on their journey and face yours. If despite wishing well those who compete with you, they still fight you, how about letting God fight for you and not be distracted from what you are called to do. This is God-kind of tactics. Where visible, engage godly tactics and lawful means to end this childish envy and resolve the conflict. A more excellent way is involving God, He does a better job at protecting His own. Remember we cannot and do not war in the flesh, which is sinful. Why pick a brash fight with another, or set traps at them to stop their hard work and productivity? It is far from riveting but revolting to good conscience. Rather, engage your rights but trust the Spirit. Let's consider Apostle Paul as citizen of Rome but a Hebrew by birth and a Christian convert, when incarcerated for preaching the gospel, breaching his rights as a citizen, he decided to invoke that priviledge. Those officers who handled him were unaware he had such honour, so quickly apologised and sought to make remedy. Sometimes you may waive your influence, but <u>there are times you may need to insist on your rights, priviledges and even call up your influence to fix some messy situation,</u> not to satisfy your ego, but to ensure good things don't get frustrated and your Christian witness impoverished. In this instance, he did not fear persecution, or necessarily wanting to flee by making sympathetic appeals, but I perceive he felt he needed to show that he had those rights all the while but for the sake of the gospel had relinquished it for most part [*Acts 22:22-30*]. There may also be times we showcase our rights, but a corrupt world may upturn it. But without question as those who hold to a Kingdom ideal, we must prove beyond doubt, our godly conscience have been exercised and that we have left a worthy testimony of our witness for the next generation. By all means, take the right path for the sake of the advancement godly and commendable objectives.

iii. Two things– on Christ as a chief mentor, and our responsibility of modelling Christ. I need to spell out that leading is being under authority but also commanding authority. To lead well the question is, are you under God to receive direction? Consider Jesus's words– Christ is the best and chief guide to have. His exemplary life dwarfs any the world has ever seen. His principles are wholesome and life-giving. When He taught love your enemies, love your neighbour as yourself, that right there was revolutionary in those days, and still is. People don't get it, they wonder what the interest is, to behave like that. Leadership is understanding the need to refuse a pattern and model of erroneous leadership, which manifests in manipulation, instigating disunity for gain, lack of mutual submission, and vices contrary to God's law. How is the greatest the one who serves or considered 'least,' in the scriptures? Humility is the word, as Christ commands love, not timidity. This calls for us to submit to His principles. So, do you want this kind of leadership? The lesser models the greater; it is saying this is how the great looks, this is what the great does. It represents effectively what is precious. The believer of Christ represents the glory of heaven, the treasure of God in the earth. The glory of God on us, the glory of God in us, the glory of God mightily at work through us. This is only so because humility is the watchword, as the one who believes in Christ has brought himself or herself to the forefront of God's agenda and is able to model the grace of God to others– God calls that person great. Everyone has the potential to be great, but we have to be His instrument.

iv.   The leadership spirit is not a destructive spirit, that destroys every good thing to make a point, or create something. Dumb isn't it? Some will say like a chicken scratches the soil for worm. But as humans there is more to do. It is getting a seed from the right source, planting it, watching it grow patiently, and harvesting it joyfully. Engaging to pick apart as default is not a right attitude, it means a deliberateness to be blind. If someone decides to profile a group of teenagers randomly in a busy street, and the instruction is– any with a green hat, stop them and search for drugs. Then someone might ask what of those with a purple hat? You agree there has to be a firm basis to that. Hats cannot be connected to attitude in all cases. Some may decide to change their hats and walk free, but without any less an intent than at first. Some may not wear hats altogether to save any long speech, questions, searches, or journey impediments. Some to make a joke may suggest a naïve and unsuspecting teenager wear one and work or walk in a dangerous search direction. Some may cheekily wear the prohibited hat knowing nothing is on them to create chaos and lay false accusations on the search party. Well, possibly, there could be the chance that a nearby group gets into a fishy deal to make merchandise of the whole situation. Whatever position you take, we recognise at some point this matter is not any longer about a hat, but much more. How a leader acts in such simple but complex situation will be crucial. One may want to connect the probabilities to the substance. The substance being that there is valid proof of chaos arising from certain detailed situations, the need to ensure lives are not negatively affected or community incited, a closer look into the symbolism of the gestures, and whether there are better ways to address the issue apart from making a bylaw for a community mass dress code which may be almost literally unenforceable. <u>There has to be a specific plan to resolve complex issues without sabotaging what is generally good</u>. Wisdom calls for care in very sensitive situations if you must bring healing to all sides.

v.   Spiritual leaders operate in 'the edge of advantage' with spiritual guidance. Simply put, the God we serve knows what happens in your bedroom. Let's consider Prophet Elisha, and how God used him to guide the ancient nation of Israel from the Syrian army, so much so it was evident that their inner secrets were being leaked out by supernatural access [*2 Kings 6:8-23*] – must have been so annoying. The secret of secrets belongs to God. It seems to me to be the case, if you have such a gift from God, He will tell you only what you should know and not all the time, according to His sovereign will. <u>If God has graced you to be directed specifically on the course to take, then you my friend have an advantage your enemy doesn't.</u> This will get you attention, as you seem to know what is coming before it does, this confuses the enemy of your soul concerning your affairs. You may be unaware, but I bet it is very annoying for those who seek to be in competition with you for no reason at all. Enjoy life, be thankful, above all get a good God direction. If any has set traps for you, that is how you soar and jump over Satan's antics and tactics. We are not all gifted in every area; as the parts of our body some are invisible to our naked eye and other parts readily seen and are left uncovered, yet all is very essential. So is the purpose of God revealed in the abilities He has given us and has enabled us with the will, life and resources to develop them. The implication of this is really wide. We ought to now recognise these abilities are for a purpose, and fully utilise it for God's glory. His glory being, His praise and for Kingdom service, also to bless others around us as well.

vi. Maximise influence to make proper recommendations. How can I use my God-given fame, wealth, position, gift and talents? And how to engage others attractively to do what is noble? How about deciding you will maximise your inbuilt giftings, perhaps yet undiscovered but need fine-tuning, and use it to uplift others. This is a proper step. There is surely a reason for the natural abilities and spiritually empowered abilities you have received- but can you tell the difference? But begin from acknowledging what you know you have and channelling it properly. What if I told you your wealth is given to you to impact others generously. For example, parents to their children, or as a philanthropist may give to others who may be in dire need. How about dealing with fame? – by using it to shine your light on an issue that may have not crossed the mind of a policy maker. Let's take another scenario, on health and beauty– how can this be a positive influence to those around you? <u>You may want to think through these and ask God to show you how you can be a godly influence with all that He has blessed you with. God has not given you any good thing as a curse. The reason He gave you that which is magnificent is so you will have an opportunity to harness it for good.</u> Esther for example in the bible was brought to prominence to the King, not just because of her eloquence, intellect or tribal affiliation, but for her beauty and grace. We know it is the favour of God– but when the time came to speak for her people who were at the risk of elimination, her beauty had placed her in a strategic place to plead their cause. God gave her boldness, and she did what was necessary. One says the story is legendary, but another discovers it is life-giving, because finding they see there is more to fleshy consummation, as God expects more. There is a purpose to your riches, fame, beauty or good name– it may seem insignificant but it's a great deal. Why do you think some persons may have it as an objective to oppose you having a positive influence or placement of any sort, it is because of the effect it can have on others generationally; you could be a force for tremendous good, that will excite any person of goodwill. It should be sufficient you seek to do good, but as King David said, he desired his enemies good, but they meant evil– weird? But this is the mystery of life. So, I urge you not to change being you, but to look inwards to what God has already blessed you with and utilise it. If any seek to stop you achieving what you earmark, would such also seek to restrain your growth? It seems so, but don't relent, God who gave can also preserve.

vii.   Leadership is service, beyond profit maximisation. Making profit is great but impacting lives positively is more durable, meaningful and better. Your life will count not for how much is in your bank account, or your worth financially, but how you served. And it is my hope you have not become numb to spiritual judgement and clarity because of the pressures of life. Did you not say you wanted to hear God's perspective on things? Well, this is it. There is a man with little who does much– by investing in a life. By no means do I mean to demonise wealth accumulation, but I am only showing you a more excellent way. What you store, definitely will come to waste– because the time span isn't forever; when you pass on from this world there is little good your wealth can do for you. Perhaps, the memory of your name? research? – except it was and is invested in people for a good cause. <u>Wealth is good, therefore receive with thanksgiving, but more importantly, use for beneficial purposes</u>. If you set up an outfit it is important you think of sustaining it through successful outcomes or profit as you may say literally, but as I argue here to show how it goes beyond profit making to impacting lives. You can say the business itself is life impacting as salaries are paid, homes are sustained, contribution is made to the national economy– you do well. How about thinking through what is being delivered by your business. Is it quality or harmful products or services? Are your employees properly served in decent wages where the business is of substantial worth? How does the goals serve in expanding godly principles? Do you now see what I see?

viii.   Eternity, the watchword. A godly leader considers how life matters in light of eternity, and so must make the most pivotal decision concerning his or her soul, and encourage others to do same. You see one's decisions cannot afford to relate to only temporary things, neither does it have to be a century long plan for your life, but it has to be a now decision that sees farther, into the future– to when you are no longer on the scene. By this I do not mean a thought on posterity, but rather a reference to the unseen realm. The bible teaches of life after the now, where each person must give an account. I stress that eternity must be on our top priority list. <u>Your thoughts on eternity will influence what decision you take now</u>. <u>This eternity–in-view kind of living is not to ignore the present, because to understand it sure adds up</u>. For the future is based on the decisions of the now. However, the decisions of the now is informed by the anticipation of future goals. Both happen to be intrinsically linked. Where there is the possibility of eternal living when the body collapses in death, how have you prepared for it? Well, we must take the bible seriously as it shows us such life exist– neither can you ignore the prediction and teaching of a book that has come true on every occasion– and that not circumstantial evidence, but true predictions. That's weighty. Beyond the accuracy of the scriptures, the living application and relevance of it, to shape sound values system and on spiritual matters, should get one thinking.

ix. Building teams and disciples with divine purpose. Christ's ministry was distinctively impressive, not only on a supernatural dimension, but it was marked with an incredible ability to work with people. People loved Him. He utilised their gifts and kept them near. Often, we see the multitudes throng alongside Him. He rebuked them on one occasion, on whether they followed Him for the miracles and food, or for His teachings. What was clear He was a good company to be with. He showed He cared after them by the way He spoke, His attitude and decisions. He will say to His disciples, 'ask the people to rest here,' 'give them some food,' 'what do you want me to do for you' and so on. There was compassion to His ministry. Incredible, interesting conversations. At times, though He came hard and rebuked those full of themselves, like some of the leaders taken aback by His teachings and popularity. He called out some men, as they were like 'white sepulchres' a reference to their hypocrisy and selective justice– beautiful grave but dead bones inside, He warned of not casting what is holy to 'swine,' rebuking those who showed disregard for the grace of God– these were 'snakes,' deceitful [*Matthew 23:13-39*]. This Jesus, what a man. I thought that did come across as fiery. Some straight talk. I wonder how many you will have left in a congregation if a preacher said these things today? The good news is that Christ has come to call all people from darkness into His marvellous light. With the Lord everyone is welcome. Christ's truth however resonated with many and it was clear to see why, given the way He lived. This manner of honesty in speech and life style gravitated the right people to Him, but also, perhaps, that was why some sought to destroy Him. Most persons are not ready to change their life or culture, especially when they think it is working just fine– it may not be the best, but we like it. That generation had a place of worship, but Christ questioned whether the law of God was operational in their heart. A leader would think how to raise a core, in friendships and associations, a team who share your vision, those you can mentor and inspire, those also you can benefit or receive from their wisdom as well, who connect on a deeper level. This synergy comes with patience but must be a necessary component and indispensable goal. Christ's spiritual style of leadership raised disciples [a committed people to His principles and life style], not just followers in name– those who only merely followed with the crowd didn't stay too long to endure the teachings. Not all who followed Christ where committed disciples, but He didn't turn them away, He gave them room to grow, and to hear and be blessed. Christ's pattern, is a called to discipleship which is true followership, not hopping along with the crowd without making a commitment to Him.

x.   Consider being enriched by lifting others up not mainly self-interest. There is something lacking in the modernistic approach to living where is basically oriented around self. Perhaps because a few have become disillusioned, and even more extra cautious to the idea of group investments or planning, because of risks, such that long term goals are often double guarded to ensure maximum personal benefits– you only have to examine options from prenups to pension plans to see how care is taken to safe guard self-interest. Some argue business partnerships may collapse, marriages may fail, kids may leave, banks may go bankrupt, friends may get new friends for new holidays, then it comes to how well you have planned for you. I think however to be so consumed by possible lapses in team efforts or institutional failures is to miss the point that scripture says two is better than one, and that God has designed life to be lived in community. <u>Hence true living has to go from living just for you to also living for others</u>. Nothing bad in taking care of you— whether by an act as simple as bathing, or something more complex as making financial investments, or protecting you, well, whatever it is, it is fine; but where it tilts towards a dicey edge of paranoia and to forgetting that a measure of giving up on some of your priviledges to earn trust and build great team goals, then there should be concern. Come to think of it, some level of trust will be required even alone, even with strangers— in terms of purchases, interactions, commitments to a secure plan. Complete isolation would be a mirage. Even canned food eaten in a secluded place in a mountain, is not so niche, or fortified exclusion. At old age, after giving up some privacy to invest in others, you may be blessed to reap such, even an institution would need to keep your terms. Think of it this way, how about I open up to love, not for a necessary financial return, but to serve a greater purpose– to God and His idea of community. Some resist the thought of this kind of supernatural influence, and disagree to following the principle, only to realise their quality of life have been enhanced by its blind observance – in some cases benefiting from the blessing of community who set out to uplift their circumstance. Only to see years later God was behind all that. Like sowing and reaping on the earth.

xi. Living and leading as one that must give account. Leadership involves developing an ethic of awareness that actions produces future responsibilities. That means there is usually the possibility of review or appraisals that will either determine a commendation or demotion. How then is a leader to live? It seems to me that sensitivity and care not to make silly mistakes is key. No one is infallible, but minimising unnecessary risks is very important. From a biblical perspective, God as ultimate judge will bring to account all of our actions someday, sometimes in this life through the turn of events that repays that ill you have done to another, or definitely when all is said, and all done. There is a plethora of stories in the bible were God allows punishment for evil in the lifetime of the perpetrators. King Nebuchadnezzar of Babylon was one of those who in the time of his reign at some point took so much pride in his accomplishments and forgot to give God thanks, he lost his mind and was brought low; when he was restored he had learnt his lesson [*Daniel 4:28-37*]. Even so is a lesson left of nations who refused to show kindness by giving the children of Israel leeway in their journey to their homeland, God didn't take kindly to this. We see God, from scriptures, also discipline Israel for forgetting Him and sent His prophets in past times to prophesy of their suffering to come for a few years– which came to pass, and again their restoration. A great lesson for us all. How then do we live our life, as one without repercussions? As one with limitless 'priviledge' to do evil? I suggest a restraint, but rather to gravitate towards that which seeks to honour God in all things, knowing that God expects an account of how we have lived these years. God is not a retributive father, who gives off his children to wild beasts to teach a lesson. But He is a God of justice and equity. Would He discipline another but not His own? Would He allow a group to sacrifice their children, worship stones and woods, engage in illicit acts, disobey Him and be unrepentant, and not act? I wouldn't think so. We see the mercy of God in perpetrating discipline, and restoration with great love, rewarding beyond and above. You ought to go do same. Adopt the character of God. His rebuke is for restoration not destruction, except where one is bent on their ways. That said, does a creator not have authority over His own? Who will say to God, why insist on your ways? Well, He is God of all flesh.

xii. Leading is not necessarily visible impact— but also 'ripples of influence.' This is why God is a just rewarder. I once read somewhere that the best and gigantic structures have firmer foundations— that would seem plausible, if it is to hold the weight. Though we don't see all that's needed to go in the ground yet that forms part of the entire stable structure. <u>All that there is, is not necessarily visible to the human eye, but could mean more.</u> For a first class global leader, you have to ensure you are mindful of this fact, and ask— 'How can I manage my visible moments and also not so necessarily tangible aspects of my life? How can I deal with areas I can control and wisely accept areas I cannot control? How can I handle stress? How can I make effective decisions before taking physical actions?' I suggest these framing are all important considerations. There are actions taken that are not always in the public purview that could affect our lives later, even those around. Something as simple as having a good diet, or drinking clean water, exercising– as everyone should be opportune to, are things which could impact on the individual's health. With a failing and frail health, their immediate family could be emotionally disturbed about this, and where there is a loss of income as a result then others who depend on them would also suffer loss. Now an individual in crisis, could spiral to cause a family to experience decline, affecting work and productivity. So even on a larger scale, some political or economic instability in some regions could threaten the peace of their neighbours. Another example, certain connections, associations, friendships could impact on the quality of your own life, it could set you up for being profiled until cleared, who knows when, and afterwards with no compensation, apology, or alternative. When someone says I wouldn't hang out with you because of your kind of unruly friends, they are saying there is a level of influence coming through they are not willing to engage with. Their profile of you becomes how you are seen. The leaders of Christ's day really wondered why He hung out with sinners of all sort, because His reputation could have been easily tarnished. Christ's response was He came to those that didn't fit their religious boxes. Make no mistake, though He welcomes all, He however had no place for those full of themselves, self-righteous folks, neither was He to be found chasing up palace appointments. In His time on earth, He was out there doing the father's business of saving souls. <u>Christ realised His connections was important, that it would bless those He met, and give an opportunity for them to review whatever misconceptions they have had before an encounter, and leave changed and going out to tell others the impact Christ has made in them. The ripples of God's grace– God changes one to transform another</u>. Often some blame God, however the wonder is whether at the start point of whatever challenge or connection, if we could take responsibility for a change and start making the right decisions– eating healthy, supporting those who can't take a necessary step, directing our hearts to human compassion like Christ did. Not turning away the orphan as routine, or mindlessly snubbing the falsely accused. Another blessedness of such a story is a situation as paying for the tuition of a poor child, or offering a loan or scholarship to support this need, where such a person meets any stipulated criteria; this could mean a few decades down the line, they are in turn able to feed a family, sponsor another child or children, or become responsible members of society that makes a worthy moral example or financial contribution. What a multiplying positive gift that will be to society. It seems strongly to me that God has set natural laws in motion for us to follow, such that preserves the rights and dignity as humans, but also goes further to set the laws of sowing and reaping, where not only seeds return a harvest of fruits, but also our deeds and intents of our heart abound with a varied harvest according to the quality of what we have invested. This may be subject to time, or a few exceptions according to the workings of His grace, but largely and fundamentally there is an outcome for every seed sown. The fruit of righteousness will produce a harvest of peace and joy— all of God's blessings in God's time.

xiii. To lead successfully, morally, spiritually is to wholly trust God's principles revealed by the spirit of Christ for salvation, to avoid catastrophe. Not trusting in your own sense of moral goodness or plans that excludes God. Simplistic? Is it? When, if you are a believer, you have detailed a five-year goal and in the place of prayer the spirit of God ministers to you to practically for all intent and purposes strike it off for a week's goal and in an utterly different direction! Then your trust is tested. Your ability to hear right spiritually is also tested. This is why, a voice in your mind could be warning you of a massive misfortune were you to take what seems lucrative but yet would be unhelpful in a long run, but rather to settle for what seems a minimised and weaker plan but yet could spell a positive turn around into tremendous success. If anyone can tell the future, God can, beyond any mind-reader or sorcerer any business tycoon can hire. Sometimes these decisions may not even be about any financial gains, but a spiritual redirection to secure your health, or prioritise your family commitments. God will stop us on our tracks if He perceives any decision would hamper His good plan for us. Is it possible God could ask something of you that will require a truly hearing ear to hear? How easy now? I suggest to you that leadership by the Spirit is more God than you. Nothing wrong with feasibility study and detailed plans, however, it is humbling when you realise that some men who fear God can conceive of more sophisticated plans but are willing to hear God show the next steps. <u>God could bless your plans and even inspire it, but sometimes He may require less from you to show His incredible power, so be sensitive</u>. As with Gideon and the battle with the Midianites, God may need less human force [*Judges 6:11-27*]. <u>The genuine leader would say, what would you have me do now, Lord?</u> Rarely do we ask if God wills we bath, eat, or fulfil some basic duties; but openness to the spirit is when you realise God may interrupt your hours, as He may need you to fast, hurry elsewhere, help someone, or simply do what you normally do as routine on that occasion– but again, as an exception, but no static rule. It is not going crazy, it's just being sensitive to the inner voice of the spirit of God. I can hardly explain this, but God help me. If you are not filled with the Spirit, don't bother because it will be your mind repeating things to your head, guesswork and then meaningless. If God is in it He may spare your life severally by asking you to take a turn, or stop an action, or desist from a fellow, or make a physically draining trip on a mission. And only when later you connect the dots and realise He literally moved you to preserve you or made you gain an experience too valuable for words. As Ananias was instructed by the spirit to go to Saul who later became Paul, by the Holy spirit's directive [*Acts 9:10-19*]. Like Philip the Evangelist who is asked to wait on a road juncture by the spirit, in anticipation of a traveller who was about to walk through, finally meets an Ethiopian a royal official under Candace the queen, and afterwards was taken elsewhere by the same spirit [*Acts 8:26-40*]. As Jesus would rest in a storm rather than be given to hysteria over the possibility of drowning. God in His mercy, which is rare often to redirect them to Himself, had spoken too to persons who were not of faith yet, and had no evidence of a spiritual relationship, sometimes in their dreams or on visit by a prophet– examples would include to Pharaoh concerning a coming famine in Egypt [*Genesis 41*], Belshazzar of Babylon who saw the finger of God making a writing on the wall and rebuking him [*Daniel 5:24*], the Roman Centurion who was visited by an Angel directing him to go call for the preacher, Apostle Peter, to communicate the gospel to him in his house, of which Peter received a confirmation to accompany him [*Acts 10*].

xiv.   There is wisdom in nature, secular outfits, but a good spiritual leader keys into the spirit realm to understand seasons and times. How can an individual understand what a nation is supposed to do? How possible is that? That a man can instruct a nation? We know that politicians or monarchical rulers have through the ages taught and told their people of options to take for progress, but however, often also falls victims of backlash when the plan fails. Rarely do unknown men even where wealthy have arisen to instruct a people. But we know that exceptionally gifted people may. I also put to you that as in Bible times prophets and spiritually acknowledged people did instruct Kings. It's by understanding season and times you're able to appropriate the advantage a period brings. It takes the help of the Spirit of God to know what to do. You may have to be still, and be at peace, when everyone around think you must now act or never do so, especially when you know it is not time. What if the voice of God was varied from that of the people? Yes, it could be, and often is. <u>The season and times I speak of transcends nature's moments– of dry and wet weather times, summer and winter, and everything in between; it's more about the</u>

ability to sense moments of opportunity than whether it rains physically. This is similar to other scenarios that may require a person to act, or not take an opportunity, as it may lead to ruin. A classic example is God working in Joseph, the son of Jacob [Israel] one of patriarchs of the Jewish nation, whilst he was in Egypt, to give an incredible vision for an economy plan that could save the nation from ruin. The put forward advisory policy was towards ensuring in a time of great stability to make extensive and imminent investments and savings [of their crops harvest], as against any ludicrous ostentatious or even priority projects, in anticipation of famine, as food security. The admirable result– they had the privilege of surviving a downturn in economic fortunes, all because of the incredible vision and opinion a young man filled with the Spirit of God gave. The key– it was timely, and yet instructive. When the famine came, other nations suffered but Egypt survived. Also, thanks to leadership that understands wisdom can be outside the palace too.

xv.   Leaders of the spirit know genuine labours are not in vain and that fruits come in their season. This mindset still fills you with perseverance. Surely your strength and willingness will be dissipated in time especially when it relates to supporting others and with no revenue in return, <u>unless you understand the benefit of times and seasons in relation to receiving a harvest, and the blessing of the process not being in vain. Labours are not in vain where channelled into relevant projects.</u> Every good worker knows this, so the season they're in becomes bearable. Understanding the season you are in, tells you to plant or harvest, or whether the conditions are right or not, or as to what to do. But however, the instinct to know what comes after that present season will ignite perseverance. 'Rain is coming' the wise would say, so I will do this or that now. This mindset also informs your present partnerships, as you will need what is glorifying to God on your journey, and what would help you get to the next level. Abraham would not need his nephew on the journey to his promise, no matter how close he was to him. He had to understand it was God at work, so had a release to bless each other, choose their inheritance, and then move in separate ways. Same with Paul and Barnabas, the one partner that had been instrumental in joining him in bringing the word to communities, yet they had to in peace move in on their spiritual journey. I suspect God wants people to work together in mutual respect, but some are not grown up to receive this, rather than people impede the work, then the best thing is to ensure decisions are made in a God-honouring way. Such that the work of God continues without unnecessary interference, hopefully in a way that grows each other and not destroy each other, or whatever team of partners. This too requires leadership, of what is best to be done in that season. There are several aspects of our life processes— often when you do deal with one, another comes up. Almost like a constant revolving circle, and you wonder whether there will ever be a time of completion of all tasks. Some have to make decisions on their mortgage payments, career, bereavement, on taking up an education, loss of friendship, travelling and holidays, investments, and so on— soon you realise that whatever your goals are you have to see if it syncs with whatever commitments you have in other places. This mainly being because the timelines of our journeys are not mutually knit. However, the key is magnifying God in each process, following His way, and not through deceit and wickedness in achieving an end, as even after your victory you feel empty. There is no need to join with the world that glorifies shrewdness and deception at the expense of the poor, rather than honour God for the favour, establishing a bleak view of God as though He only helped those who blew the rules. I know God is bigger than that.

xvi.   Spiritual leaders are open to spontaneity and intervention of the Spirit. And will be willing to take the initiative and preach the word of God anywhere, and with the example of their lives, however on certain occasion God sends willing leader where the need is greatest. We read specific instruction was given to Apostle Paul by the Holy Spirit restraining him from going to Asia but to Macedonia for the time being. God sends to a place suited for your gift, even if you don't think so. The power of choice has been given to those who are graced to listen, and in some places even if your gift is suited they may not receive you. As much as the grace of God is involved don't worry, it's not you that is rejected, it is the Lord. Who says being a leader is not compatible with being a godly witness? Be open to being carried away to whichever neighbourhood or project God wills– even if it is a stone throw away. Also, be ready to make or set aside plans, and strategies if God needs you to, only be sensitive to the spirit. Be ready to adjust your calendars to fit the schedule of the spirit. This is not to hush the fact that good progress often requires careful planning, but my counsel is be weary of careful planning alone if God is not in it. The 'horse' may be prepared, the 'house' may be built, the 'defences' may be erected, but safety is of the Lord. Whatever it is, if God is not in it, it matters nothing my friend. This scriptural perspective varies from the world's perspective. The world thinks efficiency, but the word teaches efficiency but never neglects faith either. You could read of a driver driving within speed limit, of sound mind, aware of the pros and cons, and from nowhere a crazy person decides to take a swerve that ends the life of a family– the lesson we fail to see often when we are preserved from such a horrific incident is the God-factor, that gives us the protection despite taking all the care. Of course, should we be very careful, observe the laid down instructions and take all trainings if relevant? Yes. Should we even be extra cautious? Most certainly, my admonishing is, after haven done all that is required, remember that your safety and assurance must remain in the divine– the leading of the Spirit.

xvii. Spiritual leaders are not scared to start small and are willing to invest in people with the little resources they have. I recall in my university days I recognised there was a gift to intercede for men of God and offer a prayer for our world and to evangelize Christ. Notwithstanding the limited resource I said to myself I would like to talk to as many as possible in every class. Investing in the human person is a great gift you can give. God helping me in the eight years of my undergraduate studies, especially in the later 5 years in the law programme after completing a two-year undergraduate diploma in data processing (apart from college administrative delays), I really took up the challenge in my spare time to share with my friends and colleagues the gospel. God was still teaching me but I knew I had to use the gift in me, not complain about the size of opportunity, how so grateful I did maximise it. Despite the disruptions in academic calendar in the institution at that time, there was such incredible grace to me a minister of the gospel of Christ; perhaps some would recall me speaking to them, a seed I see flourishing in a few today. I remember speaking to some brothers in the faith to join me in early morning prayers to make intercession for saints and preachers globally, didn't make much sense then to some, but I'm so glad I did, and encouraged others to. I see we were fulfilling this principle of being faithful in little. Christ has given us the priviledge to see the fruit of the gospel materialise. The message is the same, it is God's will to love all people, according to the abilities He has given us. We have a responsibility to create opportunities for the gospel, whether locally or even at a global level, if you do so using the gift you think is 'small,' God will surprise you beyond your imagination, to the extent He is willing to take you. In every God-given capacity, the focus is the same, how you can maximise that to reach others positively. As a Christian minister the message is the same, the message of God's love to all people, a calling to reach the nations with the message. Even for the person who is not a Christian, God has placed some abilities and skill in them too, which they can use for the benefit of their community– even though some are not thankful for these abilities because they think it is only 100% self-effort. <u>A spirit-based leader would acknowledge the source, and will use the gift in a beneficial way, irrespective of how little it seem.</u>

xviii. Leadership is about the leading through godly influence not just influence. I consider leadership in its entirety as positive, a great opportunity for influence– in a proper sense to utilise influence in a godly manner. Why should a bad role model or tyrant be considered a leader? And enforcer or dominating ruler do not make good leaders. Perhaps we shouldn't use, I would say oxymoronical term 'bad leader' because it is more for illustration, as a leader suggests not just the ability to only occupy a position of influence but to truly lead, and rare do bad leaders lead– no one is inspired by their 'leadership.' It is understandable why we speak of bad leadership because there are cases where you have erroneous leadership becoming a bad influence. Leadership in the truest sense is to serve, to show good discretion, to inspire, to show prowess and ability to direct and command authority. The inability to lead creates oppressors, abusers, manipulators, impersonators and opportunist. By this I do not mean one smeared with vain accusation. Some said of Christ– away with him, give us Barabbas [*Matthew 27:17*]. Christ in their opinion was the epitome of fraud, a deceitful person, an impostor of Prophet

Moses the true deliverer; yet in Him laid the future of humanity! <u>A leader or shepherd has to be distinguished from an impostor or hireling– these will forcefully compel followership through deceit and brute strength, however the leader's influence who rules in a godly way is based on understanding and love</u>. Leadership is of course beyond people's following, it is also why they follow you. Have you compelled followers by false pretence, assigned followership for manipulation, by abduction, bad influence, control and threats– these wouldn't be said to have earned your trust or you their genuine loyalty. Soon they will leave by clarity of facts and when their personal agenda is met. True leader leaves a legacy that lasts a life time. Even when all the record books are done it will celebrate true leaders. Should those in control of machinery of the state of affairs decide to omit their efforts, their influence in some way never remain erased, somehow the resurface. Certain virtues in leadership are eternal– truth and love are one of those. They resurface in their seeds, which becomes fruit. Seeds of love planted in the hearts of people. Seed that those of goodwill will find tenaciously and translocate to other appropriate quarters, so others can be blessed too by. Some may even weep when it is rediscovered and wonder what kept it away for so long. Sometimes it may appear a good thing is lost until you wait to see its reflection, its fruit, its influence and impact on someone else– leaders breed leaders.

xix. Consider standing for the truth not only when it suits you. Some say there is no objective truth and embrace a postmodernist perspective arguing from their position it is an objective stance. Really? I thought that was supposed to be relativistic. The leader has to understand it is essential for mental health itself, that there could be such a thing as a core or objective view– well, there is such thing as water, or air or you? I would think there is. Let's not be dragged into this philosophy that we cannot be sure of anything, taking an extreme view of things. I have shared with you the leader's responsibility to rule in love and to be exemplary. This would extend to being objective, not partial when required, but upholding that which is true and worthy of attestation. For the spiritual leader this is important and would consider the bible as testament of that which is true, given its proven track record. Let's not take pride in helping some seem intelligent when they boast of God's non-existence without seeking to show evidence whilst they make the claim. <u>Leaders are open to truth even when it contravenes the established popular thinking</u>. It always seems like fun fitting in, but not for long if you have to lie to become accepted. One cannot on the basis of preconceived notion barricade a school of thought and even plot its demise, without seeking to explore the merits and demerits of the stance first.

xx.   When leadership is born of love it definitely improves productivity, impact and changes lives in unique ways. Show me a person that qualifies for leadership you will find a person personified in love– I don't mean one enthroned as a dictatorial ruler, but the one who attains the virtues of love, compassion, empathy for their fellow human. Love makes a giant amongst men. <u>Your love will naturally endear you to many, because they see you have their interest at heart. Love creates positive influence</u>. Egoistic rulers are threatened by lovers, because they almost certainly distract attention from them. But even a ruler can become a leader if they begin to love. Having a position doesn't make you a leader, love will. It will influence your decision for the right causes, it would preserve many, it will cause your influence to travel beyond your reach. Love makes a way where it seems the road has become untravellable. Love gives a heart to decision making. I recall Christ saying to His disciples about His followers– that they needed to eat and rest. What an insight? This is not deep revelation making– but deep spiritual love making. These people needed affection; to eat and rest. The Lord requested they be sat in groups, and fed. But He still taught them. The balance of the benefit of the word to the spirit, and bodily care. Though God is spirit, He sees to our bodily needs and soul needs. Isn't He perfect in all of his ways? The spiritual leader understands the essence of love for God, His people, and creation [*1 Corinthians 13:1-13; John 13:34-35; Proverbs 12:10; Luke 10:25-37,38-42*]. And also, they understand how to love God in return– in hearing the word and obeying, beyond service.

xxi.   As a people of faith– can you move at God's word when He says have a go? We have this assurance of faith, that God works in us mightily by the grace of the Spirit of Christ. Leadership takes faith. Faith in the God of the

<u>process, and even beyond the process</u>. The process is often not appealing, in fact nothing in the blueprint you are going through may appeal to you, except you know the one that has called you, that He is faithful. Sometimes God may not even need a process to justify you. He may choose to skip it and bring you to the next level. However, often He puts us through the grindstone to produce a smooth flour, from the crushing of the grains. But make no idol of the process at every instance. In the bible, Enoch and Elisha didn't need to go through the process of death to get up to the next level; also, if God tarries some of us will meet the rapture whilst alive. I teach this, so you are complete in understanding. Nonetheless understand as a leader, God may need to deal with you accordingly— but work with Him in faith each step of the way, in whatever He decides to take you through. Whether it be an established route, a fast track mode, or none at all— or simply translated into another dimension. It is the same God. Your unique process may be different from another person's, nonetheless trust God in what He's taking you through. No matter what, even if some may not understand but God does. So, you say you want to be a leader? Then trust God to see

you through the process? He brings you through. If it pleases Him to the bypass any human process to lift you up, so be it. If it pleases the Lord that you are the subject of conversation at the prime minister's table, at the President's table, at the student's table, at the factory worker's table, at the street ways and byways, because of Christ, you have got to hope in His plans and give Him thanks. Because it was never about you but the God in you. Your visibility or invisibility do not matter to an invisible God, except when He says it should or shouldn't, what matters is the gospel is preached and the power of God undeniable. When God says He is going to take you to the next level, don't ask how? Or when and where? Just get ready, and like Joseph in the bible be ready to make a dungeon-palace transition, or like Apostle Paul be able to say, 'I know how to abound and abase'! How to lack and have abundance, how to be rejected and accepted. Praise God. In all, giving thanks. That will take faith as a leader. A leader able to manage your affairs and others. Understanding you may have a goal that requires perseverance to achieve. In time what is invisible will be made known by the power of the Holy Spirit. And Christ will bring all things under His reign.

xxii. Spiritual leaders are spirit-filled persons. In the Act of the Apostles, we read it was men filled with the spirit of God that was chosen to mentor and lead them. You underestimate how deficient your organisation can be without utilising genuinely Christian and spirit-filled men and women. You can also find proficient people from all backgrounds, but there is an edge of advantage these manner of persons possess, it is the ability to have insight into spiritual things in addition to whatever skillset they may possess. <u>To be a spirit leader– get ready to be a spirit-filled person. Spirituality has to accompany proficiency of skill to avoid long-term chaos.</u> As an example is a proficient surgeon without ethics as a moral compass– but I speak of something much deeper. We cannot see people as disposable cargo for experimentation. Every human has a unique gift God has put in them, and that they can offer, it behoves on those with opportunity to consider this. I just wanted to share with you a spiritual insight from the bible. Some spiritual things are not relevant to physical realities, some think it's a sleepy dream notion, a fairy cuckoo land game, or just a personal matter– nonetheless, nations make no mistake when in their prayers, anthem, business meetings, legislative assemblies the intervention of God is invited. Yet this generation has not maximised the giftings, counsel and abilities of those spiritual according to the scriptures, some have opted for evil spiritisms and stray ways, which is a counterfeit of the original, and this is very mistaken. It takes someone mature in spiritual matters to see the Christian ministry goes beyond administrative competencies, spiritual competences, and that is the grace of God. So anyone with this ability ought to exercise it for the benefit of their community. God did the nation of Israel in bible days triumph, was it by their strength alone or by the help of God? How did they reshape their moral destiny and spiritual fervour, was it by human effort or God's grace? How do we know the love and mercy of an ever living God? Who can boast in themselves and not give honour to God? To be secure you realise the need of administration but don't let it be all you have. The bible talks about becoming wise by learning from the Ants about saving in the summer against the winter. These instinct in animals is God given, how much more the human He created– and how much more the one empowered with an increased skill and spiritual ability? Such gift is for the guidance and benefit of themselves, but also others around. It seems to me God's idea is to bless the administrative leader with the Spirit's power as well, but often the split is man's arrangement or incompetence, this is a hindrance. Moses was called for the task but requested an Aaron for help with speeches, but God was already confident in Moses's ability when He called him. Also when Prophet Samuel was rejected by the people though that was not God's plan because they needed a King not a spiritual leader, He anointed King Saul who then exercise his authority in a kingly way, yet in time the nation will learn they need God all the way. King David was a man after God's heart because when he emerged he sought not only the king's administrative authority but also the presence of God as well. Gideon another of God's mighty warrior, fought knowing the presence of God and His approval was with him. The Spirit of God is not only in physical strength alone, it excels in knowledge and wisdom too according to the grace He supplies– beyond human skills of geometry and any form of creativity. What we call mere human skill is also the gift of God, harnessed through training. But how many acknowledge God in this? I speak more in a broader context of the workings of spiritual ability and grace, that channels in a supernatural dimension into earthly affairs, as we saw in bible times. This happens through prayer, as we pray God's will to be done on earth and in us wo believe. It is the ability to know when to apply it, and how to apply to save a nation— by divine insight. Do I speak again of the bible story of Esther? Whose beauty would charm a nation and bring her favour before royalty but knew the grace of God was not something to shied away from but was a gift to redeem her people. In fasting and prayers, God working even through her beauty, she brought blessing to many in her time.

xxiii. Spiritual leadership is about bearing responsibility for the preaching of the word of faith and being intentional to seeing the glory of God revealed. The believer of Jesus Christ is graced with the ability to be a spiritual leader. To lead his/her affairs in the fear of God, family, friends, the group where he finds himself, to lead their community ushering in the presence of God, even providing this manner of influence to those he or she may not know, near or far. But you will have to take responsibility for this. I hardly know a person operating fully and authentically in spiritual dynamism and exposed to the nations or groups of influence, that is not graced with the ability to communicate the word of faith. Simply put, they must have heard God to represent Him. It is like sending for a David from the sheep's pen, or a Moses arising from the back side of the desert, or a Gideon coming forth from his vineyard, or even a John the Baptist staying wait in the desert, until it is time for the spirit to reveal them to their respective generations, and their preaching of the word of faith in a God bigger than themselves. You cannot talk of a God you do not know. You may talk about Him on the presuppositions of another or a third party, but that is not a lived experience, it takes spiritual leadership to be ambassadorial and be one who presents a real experience of God, not a documentary about Him, because you could be remove from such an experience. The spiritual responsible leader has a calling to reach out to those around them with the manifold love of God. The leader has a responsibility to showcase Christ to their world. Not only in conduct but in their testimony as well. As a spouse we not only love in action alone but in true and affirming words, nor will affirming words be sufficient if no motivating action. This is true in this instance. Even so our words will motivate action in us and others. In my ministry I meet people often from several ethnic backgrounds with very divergent ideas of what God represents, and some speak passionately about what it means to them to hold this opinion then often seem to deflate when I ask them what they will do if they hold on to it so dearly, and yet discover it is not true. That is the problem of any conviction you have, it has to be based on any verifiable fact. Don't be taught by emotion that you lose sight of truth, with the eyes that faith gives, not physical eyes but more than that, spiritual eyes. Passion has to be based on solid evidence, on truth, sincerity, love, on that which is proven overtime. If God is with a person He bears witness to their words or teachings with unexplainable supernatural signs and wonders, and miracles, according to His ability. I don't mean coincidences, but divine 'God-moments' where you perceive strongly and often clear this has to be God at work, because no way in the world of human effort or natural course of events could you have done that– because that is above the natural.

Satan tend to seek to make counterfeits of God's testimony, as if to rubbish it, but see God's work and grace is tested and is strong to all who believe in Him, committing to His leadership. This is the gospel of forgiveness and love we preach to those especially willing to encounter God. And together with others who witness God's grace and affirming power, it is to know that only God can pull that off- the supernatural.

xxiv. There is no need to take advantage of perceived weaknesses of others. How about strengthening the weak to be more efficient? Yes, and focusing on your own strengths. You are truly at race with your own person, your own dreams, objectives– come to think of it, what's the point achieving another's goal that won't make you happy. You desire to copy because you have not discovered you, and your unique you. You can be inspired by another but not to be their carbon-copy, sample, or fake. The best counterfeit is not the original. A leader would understand this and not be enticed or covet another's presentation– like Cain. It takes maturity to attain that height, when others can inspire you and you are not mad about it or to wish such to be non-existent. Leaders would rather uphold fairness than fan an evil perception of another to get any possible direct or indirect affirmation. Their energy is not boosted by the fall, neglect or weariness of another. They are strong and show up because they have to do so consistently and have a genuine reason to. How sweet it becomes where you are the mature one in a conflict, you relax your insistence and let matters lie in peace– not often many can do this, especially if exploited and your weaknesses puts you in a difficult situation, or perceived weakness derail the respect due to you, or becomes a medium for attack or for domination, rather than support and upliftment. Even your help could be seen as an attempt to curry favour– and the generous person goes 'what? I just meant well!' There are those who notice you greet them first in your office, and then get offended the day you don't – and you wonder should I always now do that first? What happened to mutual spontaneity? I think a leader should recognise people's generosity and appreciate them, no matter how little. Because often they show it even if they don't have to. Well, decency and a good conscience is to not take advantage of another's good conscience, or what the world thinks is weakness, in not being brash or vile, or to master over another. Rather consider reciprocating goodness with love and thanks, and also supporting the weak. Consider Christ- He was friend of sinners, yet King of righteousness. What a balance, what a life. His life was positioned to lifting others up. It was as if He wasn't intimidated by their well doing– He wasn't. Why should He? His goal was not to look better by disassociating Himself or highlight the weakness of others to their shame but for their repentance, but He would often rebuke the self-righteous. If you find this principle too difficult, then again consider not doing evil or being passive about doing good. You will think this is common sense, but it will amaze you how many people think of and generate mental energy for their degenerate business or any wickedness of theirs, by despising and putting down others. You never know how powerful the reverse of this is, can be, which is helping those deserving, until you do. I would think it dumb to be oppressive and abhorrent.

xxv. The ability to continue to work together with those who you have influence over in unity requires a great deal of leadership, rather than being in denial of their relevance to you. Why divide a team against itself to keep it together? This would not be wise on the long term. Leadership requires the deliberateness to create conditions that ensures pulling together with the force you want to work with. When others are not willing to do so when they don't have their way, you should ground your decision on a sound basis, on why it is better to work as a team, except where it is preferable not to. It is not always about cherry-picking an individual's demands but what is best for everyone you have responsibility for– than being self-centred. When you own this spiritual principle, it informs your personal choices. Especially the choice to work with others in peace and tranquillity, other than being a catalyst for hate. There are those who stir up strife where there is none, to ensure you keep your distance from them – is that even possible? Or is it just an illusion some people could be like that and really try to cause dissension? Well, read the *Psalms* you will see King David reiterating that some do cause trouble for no cause. Perhaps just not to be close, or to associate with you, or be with you. Not because you have wronged them, but just they prefer to be that way, or perhaps because you have no benefit to them. I think a really deep response is to choose to be a priviledged person to others who may need to know you value their input in your team, than forcing unwilling persons, or seeking to be unhelpful yourself. Choosing not to agree when there is need to, is not a reason– by reason, is a reference to substantive causation. Something reasonable at least, whether that is justifiable is another matter– but to say simply 'I don't like the look of another,' 'I feel apprehensive around,' 'I don't just know, I think such a person is evil.' This is not the way to live life, there has to be a genuine concern to decide not to work with another as a leader. Your threshold for tolerance has to be deeper, to work with people who are not like you, or eat what you eat, talk how you talk, dress how you dress, with personal differences or a wide range of varied experiences, the harmony and similarity should focus on the objective or task you envision together, which could work for a common good. This resolve takes discipline to accomplish rather than fluctuating emotions or brute decisiveness. To sever partnerships of influence, those involved ought to have shown unworthiness in their actions, and even then, discretion has to be that the task could not be achieved uncompromised. This is not about a right not to dispense with any in your team or maintain a team whilst snubbing them right under your wings, its putting a human face to leadership, a heart touch to decision making. God will not be pleased if people are treated as an animal and hurdled up, such that they don't feel they belong, or where they are completely unessential, and yet they are forced to coexist. It is a chronic minimalisation of responsibility to choose not to be neighbourly in our relations. If it is a phobia question, a sense of personal trepidation, a question of perhaps of need or purpose, it would be much more understandable than as a preference to segregate one's self from another because you think they are too important for you, or not at all, or because you have to be put in a situation with someone who doesn't share your physique or psychic. To be a leader begin to decide to broaden your horizon to be inclusive, so you can harness potentials from a richer range, but remember not at the expense of core values. I espouse on real unity of purpose. The more one grows older you will discover there is a gift in everyone you meet, it may not be what you expect, but be patient so you will find their raw gold- a treasure, which you may not benefit from but some may. The goal becomes not one's selfish goals but how by working on it you can produce something that makes the person, or you, the better for it. This is somewhat mentoring. That's leadership not just being a colleague, business person, stranger or even a friend– leadership is more, it is pulling strengths together for a purpose greater than self-interest. And it starts with those little pockets of influence you have, making the right decisions here and there, to integrate people, achieve goals and leave others better than you meet them. This willingness to work in unity and engage with one another must not be confused with a sense of 'therapy' you get from wanting to be away from anyone for a bit of time– as Christ in some occasion actually will withdraw from the crowd for some calm and meditation. You will need that. There is no need to feel guilty when sometimes things are so intense, and you just need some space– I've heard it being called, some 'me time.'

xxvi. Think– how can I make the next generation better? <u>Leaders think how they could raise the generation after them to be better than them, in fact it is a joy to grow the next generation of leaders.</u> Sometimes it's about passing the baton, other times it is about raising leaders to work alongside. For the coming generation to be fully equipped they will have to learn to serve, to train either as an apprentice or have opportunities for first-hand experience about what leadership is all about, and this does not have to be formal. This could be opportunities to watch the leader in their normal course of operation in leadership so they learn the ropes, observe interactions and character, and receive the necessary affirmation needed. Spiritual leadership is not empowering a group of insecure and unwilling men or women who think becoming a leader like their mentor is 'dethroning' their protégé, to become the 'next big thing,' or entering a competition of who is the greatest. When I observe that manner of attitude, I wonder what is all this about? Because it is so weak a mentality. You don't have to be obsessed by whose turn to take the credit or who is to now direct the turn of events. The overwhelming concern should be how can I keep preparing for the task and serve tenaciously. The person is weak who thinks it is true to suppress a leader suspected to be out to destroy their ambition without proof– the question is, why not let God fight for you? Also, why not ensure you find loyal and willing people to 'lay hands on' [authorise], not a mischief maker who seeks to usurp authority. Often sound leadership ethics is skewed in modern life, social media, and even on some TV shows so the young aspiring to leadership may pick up very bad habits that may be repugnant in their real and practical situations. Also understand God's style of leadership is in some cases very countercultural and may challenge you to love when there is so much hate and envying around. Trust God to teach you how to be resolute but yet gracious– you will need both. You must have patience as a leader, and be one led of the spirit, so you can find the right people for the spiritual kind of leadership and develop them, rather than picking people suddenly. It must not necessarily be one from your street or tribe, neither does the excuse for this always has to be 'grace found them,' you will hope the grace of God can also find someone you have no ties to you culturally, as it seems the reference to the grace of God has to be genuinely spirit-led inspiration, and one selection based on love and soundness of character. This is not to say that you will not find a lovely person from your cycle of friends, family and even your culture, but be sensitive to God's voice. Spiritual matters must be handled with much openness to the preferences of the spirit.

When you find the right person invest in them, what God has taught you, even as you recognise your limitedness and the fact that those you train today may turn out more blessed than you. This is fine, as a true leader wishes this to be the future, for the next generation to exceed their expectations or landmarks– so long God is glorified. This is because a protégé's blessing in the faith from their spiritual father, is also their spiritual father's blessing. Just the same way we who believe in Christ have His blessings, and He rejoices over us without rivalry, and He even wishes we do greater works than He did on earth. We have become children of God by faith in Christ. A spiritual offspring's responsibility, as son or daughter to a spiritual leader, is to recognise their father's contribution to their progress, send appreciation, support materially as opportune for their own blessing from God, intercede for such as their mentor through their prayers, and also be a ready ally in times of conflict. A grown offspring is like a preservation and help to their leader. It's a responsibility but a joy to watch those raised up in the faith become useful, not wayward. Spiritual leadership has nothing to do with Christian denominational lines or having a relationship that requires the physical presence of the mentor all the time, but a recognition you have been adopted and you submit of your freewill in godly honour to learn from them all God has taught him or her [as a spiritual father– a reference to both gender, as sonship in the bible refers to both gender as well. For more clarity you may use spiritual father, spiritual mother, spiritual daughter, spiritual son; this all refers to those who are being taught the word of God, and those who whilst in mutual biblical relationship have authority over you in the Lord and desire more deeply your spiritual growth and see to it– this goes past being a teacher to being a father in the gospel, *1 Corinthians 4:15, Titus 2:1-8*], so as a leader they can impact you too. The body of Christ is in need of more fathers, sincere men and women, who want to see this generation and the next one become spiritually strong in Christ. And true leaders have regard for mature sons connected to them everywhere and seek to invest in them for God's sake and to fulfil their heart's desire to see the work of God continuing by sharing what they have received from the Lord with these ones under their care and tutelage. If you have a child in the Lord, you should be aware, except where they are not able to contact you, but when they are able to, to bless them– as with your resources put out, ensure they have been feeding right and developing. It is good for it to be such in a defined church context, but recognise God may bless someone through you from afar. Also, a biological child could also be your spiritual child, if they are in faith and are inspired by your spiritual impact. The bible mentions of Evangelist Philip, one of the men of faith full of the Holy Spirit chosen to share food in the Church [*Acts 6:3*], but also had an incredible ministry across his community, also had children that had an inkling to spiritual matters, it seems to me there had been an impact at home to raise them towards godly reverence [*Acts 21:8-9*]; contrasted with the Apostle Paul and [Bishop] Timothy relationship which was not biological but spiritual as a father and son [*1 Timothy 1:2*]. It is important to have regard of the anointing of the Lord, to be loyal to a righteous cause, to weigh carefully every advice you receive from anyone so you are not led astray, it would not be an excuse to God that someone who was supposed to be a mentor gave an unhelpful advice; part of attaining maturity yourself as a leader is ability to discern what to receive and to honour the Lord above man. In Christ there is neither male nor female, or ethnic differences, we are all heirs of God with Christ according to the promise made to Abraham to be father of many nations and children of faith [*Galatians 3:7-9*], so let those who hope in the Lord live in the fullness of their heritage. This definite call to raising leaders as we see in Paul's admonishing to Timothy, is for faithful people. Those who will in turn transmit what they have received to other faithful people so the positive circle of this training for spiritual leadership continues for the profiting of the Church and the Christian community. To faithful men and women, signifies a deliberate cropping of honest, passionate and focused generation. It begins with recognising you have this option as a Christian to exercise this responsibility of raising godly people. In your home, godly children, in your Church a contribution to joining efforts for the young ones' realisation of their potentials, this also extends to community, where there should be a responsibility for good governance and citizenry, but this has to also mean a commitment to these principles. In relation to a Church context, understand some may pose as faithful who are not, and may come to spy the grace of God in fellowship, do not receive such as one body of Christ but thorns. There will also be those who will generate spiritual errors and blasphemy against the name by which they are called, having no desire to honour Christ, from these refuse to engage in investment of depth of spiritual relationship and leadership nurturing, as they may later turn and rend you, rather be wise and ask God how and who do you want me to invest in and the season He wants you to do this.

xxvii. 'There was a Moses before a Joshua.' How so true is this preceding statement. There is need to recognise the efforts of the past, as a blueprint and landmark, for designing the future paths. Some years ago, I heard my dad teaching on there was a Moses before a Joshua, laying spiritual emphasis for loyalty in the body of Christ, and on need for mentorship and empowerment by grace of mentorship, and also of recognition of the labour of love of predecessors. Thinking back now over the years those words still are so profound. It is through the ministry of my dad I receive Christ and dedicated my heart to the Lord, haven grown up with a Christian heritage, and experienced the baptism of the Holy Spirit, and he would later teach me about being baptised by immersion of water later in my teenage years, which I did commit to seeing it was according to scriptures, by the grace of God. I highly regard his and my mother's contribution as my biological parents and also their spiritual influence and mentorship, especially in those formative years. Also, I thank God for other men of God, some of which I presently have direct contact with, for also being a father in the gospel. <u>There are many people you owe your spiritual development and ability to walk and continually learn spiritual principles to, I suggest you have to be grateful for their influence over you</u>. But it doesn't end there you have to be a blessing to others too. As I say to people, anywhere I am priviledge to teach in, in the places God has granted me grace to. It is not enough to grow up having an idea of God without a deliberate decision to follow the Lord, but also then to give thanks for those God has impacted you by. And whatever you become, learn to thank God for the seed sown in you, and for the instruments used; however, the responsibility is on you to continue in what you have been taught, and to set the word of God as your compass for life. God will reward them in due time but also honour God in honouring them. I can attest myself the delight I have in hearing the testimony of a life touched by my ministry, or of another who write saying they consider me their mentor. I always give thanks in my prayers, and urge them to consider the word of God always. It is an honour but also a labour of love. And yes, remember, there was a Moses before a Joshua. You will however have to take personal responsibility for the outcome of the direction of your life, and not apportion blame if things don't turn out as you planned. Having counsel from any is good but weighing it up with scriptures is honourable and wise. We all would need a good reminder someday, this is where mentors can be very supportive. The emphasis on loyalty as a vital component in spiritual leadership requires more teaching in the area of detachment from fatherly leadership in an ungodly manner, to set up one's authority in another sphere that may require fatherly authority– that is speaking against all forms of rebellion. The key is not to destroy where you are leaving or left, and not despising the grace of God at work, and also for the one who leads to be ready to release others to go flourish when mature and sent by the Spirit on a mission. Some persons result to despising their trainer and leader to establish their own authority amongst doing other things, and to show the leader is no longer needful– they are the new trend in town, the new repository of knowledge, this is not wise. Why go the way of Absalom, Judas, Gehazi, Sanballat, Tobiah, Haman, Korah, Dathan, Abiram? There is a better way to go. Consider other biblical examples of Abraham and Lot, Paul and Barnabas, Jesus and John the Baptist, Esau and Jacob, sometimes you have to leave some friends or partners to go pursue your purpose, but do so amicably by choosing to head in a different direction to avoid conflict and preserve what you have to preserve. Avoid tearing down what God wants you to build up. God-kind of leaders don't deliberately cause dissensions, to cause blockade with a person or group they consider offer no considerable option to their material needs. Think as Christ would, extol values of spiritual fellowship, mutual respect, and honour those God has raised amongst you for your deliverance and spiritual growth.

xxviii. Be a God pleaser, beyond 'man praise.' Conflicts do happen, but your sanity will be, thinking 'how is God honoured above all my counterparts, in this.' Also, those with you will be thankful you took this higher call, because God's way is not necessarily man's. King David was one of those men who we read of in the Bible who was a God-pleaser. What a man. By the help of the spirit and mercy of God, he rose to kingship. What makes a shepherd boy rise to the place of Kings? What distinguishes a young man such that the head of the enemy of his nation was at his feet in battle, even though he was much younger than his adversary and inexperienced [David and Goliath challenge]? He was such that was first careful about what God thought of him first, before anything else. He would often in prayer ask God what to do, 'should I pursue my enemies, or do I stay?' There was no sense of entitlement of victories, it had to be God or God alone, his victory was of the Lord. You are not a God pleaser if your action is based on the fear of man, rather than faith in God. The two don't mix. Fearing God means not fearing man. <u>Fearing God means loving your fellow man, and not making their opinion your watchword above God's. God has to be first resort and last resort.</u>

xxix. <u>Spirit-styled leaders give room for people to change and recognise them when they do or put an effort in towards turning a new leaf.</u> You cannot unhealthily and inflexibly profile a person, permanently based on past experiences. It may serve as a guide, and please don't ignore the caution, it will save you headaches or calamity, but be willing to engage afresh and rebuild with them when you see a change of heart. This may mean staying sanctions and lifting cautions. God often was grieved concerning Israel– and said that He would disciplined them and send them into captivity. And yes, God sent His beloved people, the apple of His eyes, His firstborn into bondage of heathen nations that didn't even fear God. Why would a loving God do this? The question is why would an all-powerful God be disobeyed? Why rather, would a loving nation set itself up for punishment, by being disobedient? God has to then subsequently balance his love and justice. A lesson for us too. Consider 1 Peter 5:18-19. He is too *just* to approve wickedness, yet too loving to allow suffering to endure because of sin. Here we find the outrageousness of God's love and mercy. He knows to what extent we can bear. This do not relate to pain by persecution, even in that, God sees and will not acquit the wicked, but He will comfort His own with peace and a just reward. The real issue is, we must follow the Lord's footsteps and ensure will love again. Forgive again. And give our trust again. Not keep people in a place where they cannot know they are forgiven. However, we learn from God that in our walk of righteousness those who in time have been faithful, command His attention. We all are in need of His mercy and must be willing to show mercy. We are all servants at His service, but we do not all share the same grace, so each moment minister according to His measure of grace released to you. Yet I say this in addition, that we are all equally loved, and equally opportune to kiss His feet again and again. God said concerning Abraham– will I hide anything from him? To Moses He would say come close. To Peter, James, and John He would reveal a dimension of His glory at His transfiguration and communed literally with the heavenlies. I tell you our rewards is revealed in glory at consummation of all the things, and all who believe will share heaven's joy, yet we all would receive our just rewards. So, let the faithful continue to be refreshed in Christ's peace.

xxx. Leaders understand that God's best can be despised by some. You can be God's best, or better put, called of God to minister His grace in a specific situation, according to His sovereign discretion, yet face rejection. Many need to understand that God's best is just

grace and a person sent. We are all His best–
but be utilised for the purpose made so that
can be seen. The world had Jesus but crucified
Him and was looking to get someone else.
Leaders recognise the gift in others and are
thankful for that in them, in that relevant
time, as a word timely spoken. So, you want to
be a great leader? Be a serving leader, to all,
to the strong and to the weak, to the
oppressed and rulers, to the poor and rich, to
people of all tongues and cultures, to the sick
and well, to love those who have a voice and
those who can't find theirs. Christ was not
called to only one group– He was called to the
world. He was born in Israel for a reason but
purposed for the nations, that all might live
spiritually, but they had the option to receive
Him, and so do we today. We can criticise
those of that time for the decisions they made,
how about you today? Do you despise God,
knowing what you know from the scriptures
and access you have? As Christ ministered to
the Jews in His days, He was clear they were
children of Abraham, heir to the promise of
God to Abraham, as God's firstborn, those to
whom the revelation of God came by grace.
Nonetheless, the Gentiles were also welcome,
the Greeks, the Romans, all tribes, in and out
of Jerusalem were welcome to hear Him and

make a decision for God. Christ's teaching was bold, and still compelling today. He instructed His disciples to go to all the earth with the message of God's love available to one who believes, who do not despise it. As a spiritual leader the ball is in your court to take this message as well to the world. If for some reason you are limited in space to your community, that's not your fault, but you can minister there as well, reaching all you can reach. Some have fallen into error to minister only to a fragment of their community, and some even consider reaching a fragment within a fragment. And some even feel if a minister doesn't do this, he or she isn't called, or exciting, or belong to them— as they ought to be specialising? What is that about? Specialising, to what part of a community they preach to? It is one thing to be in a place where you are not pressed with varied attention, however the approach should be ministering to all, turning none away that is contrite and seeking the Lord. Friends, I mean well, and I hear clearly on this matter, by God's grace. <u>Begin to be a leader by becoming spiritual not carnal-minded, as Apostle Paul admonished the Church at Corinth. Who is Paul or Apollos? All servants of God, he told them, so we cannot be divided in leadership</u>

preferences, picking members we want to see according to faces, or picking leaders we want to hear in same manner. If you do this, it is God you are despising, not the individual or individuals before you. Would you prefer a man speaks in an agreeable way and you hear, even if God is not in it? Or would you prefer a man speaks in an agreeable way or perhaps, not so soothing, but you are sure God is in it, so you hear and so what is said? If God is in it, love is in it, I assure you. It is needful to discern rightly.

xxxi. To be spirit-led is to know that you take responsibility for what you feed on spiritually. Refuse forced feeding of junk that clog your soul. You try your best to put checks on so toxic information don't get in, but constantly update to the word is necessary. Especially as the devil, who is the chief antagonist of the soul is working actively through some humans, and keeps modifying his tactics but usually same evil. Nothing new really, only adapted ways, so be steady with the word and discern what is best. A leader is formed and known by right words. Why do you think people have to be trained for leadership– it is so the right words can get into their soul and cause a transformation. How do you think a person turns out if taught to hate or segregate– that person will turn out badly when in a place of authority, they will not lead but rule as with brute force and oppress. <u>To lead is to care. But to grow as a spiritual leader keep learning, don't stop learning the right stuff, not junk. Good information that will help you manage any project God gifts you with. Draw people alongside that will help you grow and take the next powerful leap of faith.</u> People that will not beat the air but help you focus on your call and how to maximise it.

xxxii. It is important to understand that discouragement and pains are sometimes God's way to teach us our limit, so we can be more dependent on Him, not ourselves. Does our body not tell us not sleeping for many days, or working too hard for a long time without rest, could lead to headaches and stress? God's polite way of telling us, to take a break and rest– through the inbuilt biological mechanism in us. Then pain becomes somewhat a warning sign, but need not be so if we took the initiative to proactively take rightly paced steps and manage things properly. If a needle pricks you, you react. Thank God you do, else it would be your body is unresponsive to stimuli which would not be ideal, as you can't tell pain or not, or what safeguards to take. God has designed things this way for a reason and a lesson. Don't be those who keep pursuing extremes for thrills, as though it is a test of bravery, maturity, resolve or godly skill; I think moderation is essential, or a reasonable level of risk is commendable with necessary safety measures. <u>First identify God–given limits and stay within your zone</u>. Where confines are not essential then pass them, else kindly be at rest with yourself. If you can't lead yourself in choices like this, how can you lead others? Discern well. There is power in operating in boundaries of grace, of decency, and not to put yourself through unnecessary risks, it may not seem so at first, but it is worth it.

xxxiii.　　What is your gift? Consider not just natural abilities, but what God has called you to do and be. People say your circumstance and natural provisions always point the way to your calling, but not always the case, though sometimes– it takes a person with spiritual insight to understand it is more about sniffing out God's specific call for you which may not look like anything you are right now, or have done, and trust Him to then walk in it. <u>Also choose to desire not wanting to be anywhere else apart from where God's purpose is at work, even when not comfortable or preferable or even seems lazy, because you think your potential in God is more</u>. Be established in the fact God knows best, especially when your will conflicts with His. Yes, you play sax very well, but what if God needs you in bible training and ministry? Or wants you to use it still? Or drop the music path altogether. It is about hearing God, saying yes to His purpose as He reveals per time. In one moment He says to Abraham, there is a place I am taking you, no exact 'postcode' or direction and details of the journey, but that He will show him. And He brought His word to pass. Do we speak of the Jesus-Lazarus encounter, He said to his family, I will be with you shortly but meant for a few more days late, but Christ needed him to be well dead before the supernatural intervention occurs, so He could demonstrate His power over the grave to all in that time, and now. God can be a bit vague, or detailed if He prefers, but walk with Him, patiently, by and by you will discover in fullest detail the plan He has for you– perhaps you can comprehend the fundamentals now, but as you journey along, more will be released to you.

What you should consider is where would He have you move– figuratively speaking, Macedonia or Athens? Prayer and perseverance with God will show you, as God can speak, it is hoped as a leader you can hear. That's what being a spiritual leader is all about.

xxxiv.   <u>Spiritual leadership is knowing you do not need crowds to effect God's purpose– not by human strength but by God's mighty hand. Also know this, God can save by a few or by many if He chooses to that way [*1 Samuel 14;6*]</u>. Like He also did with Gideon [*Judges 7:7*]. Crowds may boost your income, but the right network will facilitate your spiritual call, and if the Lord permits it will also boost your finances, making you sustainable for the long haul. God will and has always provided. But don't be tempted to join hand in partnership with the wicked, who has no regard for God. Is there still no remedy in God's house, by His principles? There is. We have to find it. God's way is higher, God could use people past their limitations. It is like a film at the theatre, telling a story, there we see all kind of ideas and often subtle setting of standards removed from Christ's spiritual doctrine, yet God calls us to a righteousness higher than that of the

'Pharisee,' whose praise and repentance is to be seen of men, but neglects the will of God. This call and grace to function is found in Christ. I must reiterate seek to please God always, not the perception of others, even 'your crowd,' those who are supposedly for you.

xxxv. It is important to know what to say and when. Best words can calm hearts genuinely without having to manipulate another. This is actually wisdom– when to apply knowledge, even how to articulate it. When to be silent, is also part of it. King Solomon, a man of wisdom, had understanding about this, and talks about knowing when to refrain from speech [*Ecclesiastics 3:5*]. Trust your conversation will benefit those who see the value of it, so it is not a hindrance to important relationships that God will open up to you. If you invest time and energy in talking with the right people you will become more confident in your dreams, if you do the opposite you will begin to deflate and may not be able to tell how that came about. So, safeguard your heart and your mouth, and you will protect your dreams a great deal [*Genesis 37*]. Wisdom will make the wise wiser. We always thank God for the grace of the early saints, but as an example we need to consider their conversations and learn, it was filled with grace. God takes interest in them, almost as though eavesdropping on you [*Malachi 3:16*]! In a loving way, for your good. There are those, no matter what you do, who will always criticise you, be careful of such. Be a person who can be open to learn from anyone where they are not contravening God's code for life. Pride has almost edged a generation from the blessedness of the gospel, and we have to be careful that as those called to leadership we keep coming to the cross of Christ placing our trust in that which the blood of the lamb has secured for us. Never be tempted to think the bible is unimportant because you heard a colleague, friend or stranger say, if God's word was so important it would have featured your community or city in the holy writ, how elementary an excuse. But conversations could get this absurd. It would be your turn to assure those you talk to that the word of God is not a play book, but a combination of resources put together by the help of the Spirit for our spiritual development but also our moral fortitude. I would encourage you that God had you in mind, and knows you by name, and He also wants you to know He saw you before the world began and His intent is good for you. When He encourages or corrects one, His heart is also for all. Through Christ we have become spiritually wiser than others, because we understand heavenly realities, yet in a measure, and only because of Jesus. This I dare to suggest to you, is true for all who wholeheartedly trust Him.

xxxvi.	Spiritual leadership is about washing feet like Jesus did. A life of service? Can we sense by correcting others in humility, we wash the stains on them, covering them, no matter how dirty rather than pointing from afar their fault. It is said to point one finger is to have four at yourself. We recognise that unless that God saved us and gave us shoes and covering our nakedness by the clothes He gave us to wear, through the preaching of the gospel, we do not only have stains but sores and shame. It is removing the hindrance in a brother's eyes only because we see clearly in ours– that by the grace of God. Without that a big fat log lies in ours to the extent that we claim to see what lies, but don't only a highly deflected vision. Maybe the fault of others were not as broad as we claimed, but for the obstruction. <u>The humility of Christ teaches, that people are drawn to compassionate hearts</u>

who are more eager to provide solutions than accusations [*Matthew 5:9*].

xxxvii.　Be able to draw from spiritual instructions to break bitter circumstances and circles. By faith Elisha injected salt in a jar and released it into the water in Jericho to bring freshness and sweetness, refreshing the people [*2 Kings 2:21; also Moses blessed the waters at Marah, throwing a tree into it Exodus 15:25*]. When God says do something, do it, it will produce positive results. By faith Moses led a people and broke a circle of oppression that lasted 400years. God so reversed it that the oppressor saw circles of affliction and plagues, one after the other, ultimately recognising that something had shifted beyond human control or normalcy, and that it was futile fighting as God was fighting alongside them. It became– 'off you go, and take some help with you.' Basically, they realised they cannot obstruct the worship of Jehovah. Don't listen to those who say it is futile serving God, rather keep listening to God, He will come through for you, and empower you to make decisions that will break off bitter derision.

xxxviii.   Spiritual leaders recognise their wealth is not for creating wrong partnerships and idols– false role models. You have an incredible priviledge as a leader for raising a new generation of influence and of power. Rather than pointing to a wrong direction for observing people, to maximise profits, how about a construct that makes for honest dealings. Some for example sell fake stories, why not consider investing in the future of young people? Even if that will not give you the 'fame,' ask for ability to maintain and to find connections that will not only bring the best in financially, but that can help make you better, and others better than you found them. A concerted effort must be made to make meaningful relationships, that will strengthen your arm– however, God must be in it. Never sacrifice the principles of God for gain, that way you set an ungodly example: see the Elisha-Gehazi story.

xxxix.   Spiritual leaders understand it is not about compelling followership or friendships, especially were they make overt and subtle attempts to severe their bond to you. Respect that. To be a spiritual leader, you will have to deal with people who think they are better off without your leadership, or that your presence limits their aspiration, or chooses not to consider your wisdom, as perhaps some unspoken rule punishes an association with you. Even Christ's leadership was considered defective by some in His time, one not worthy of upper class connections– but He was able to say His Kingdom was not of this world [*John 18:36*], and that those who followed Him was a gift from God not one of compulsion [*John3:35; 6:37; 3:16*]. But this is my counsel, where such attitude has arisen, bad if it does exist, as you may have observed, give thanks to God because they do not share in your sufferings in Christ but that God has granted you grace to share in Christ's sufferings. There is great commendation of the spirit for those who follow God's instruction all the way. We all may have this experience. But remember there are areas you can still grow, so be patient with your associations. Everything is not gold. It may be that God has saved you from a future disaster by helping you see others' true colour now, whilst you have an opportunity to. Where you have the opportunity to choose less but with joy, to have less but Christ, opt for that which is truly richer. Where you have God you have all the blessings life can bring. Shadrach, Meshach and Abednego were righteous young men in the bible account who had the favour and fear of God, and said if God does not deliver them yet they will still serve Him. Their honour for God was genuine. And like Job said, He will trust God even if He slays him [*Job 13:15*]. Knowing God can be trusted with His goodness and will not bring him to any harm. God cannot deny Himself. You must believe God has power to fix any situation working through you. Difficult times shows you life's frailties and why you need to anchor all your hopes on God even more.

xl. Spiritual leaders understand their responsibility to their own generation in righteousness in faith towards God. As we contrast Exodus 32 and Daniel 3, one generation understood they were not raised for such a time to follow the crowd, but to stand out for God. God regretted over another generation that ignored Him and murmured, and He was set to consume them; but to the three who stood firm on His word, He stood with them. He stood with them in the midst of their conflicted situation, in the midst of the wider context of their captivity, so neither caused them harm. The call to deep rooted Christianity is not just a call to moral codes observance but to the knowledge and submission to the authority of Christ, where our worship then becomes of love in faith [*Philippians 3:7-11; Romans 10*]. It then becomes necessary because of Christ to be responsible in our dealings, to avoid that which bends into recurring addiction or overwhelming focus on self or group reliance, rather than in Christ which has the potential to spring in you a love for others. The motive for our choice to trust Christ becomes honouring God, rather than the trappings of religion [*Romans 14:21*]. Even in the minutest detail it becomes good to ask God– how does my eating meat, 'veg,' drinking, abstinence or lent-like practices, dancing, exercise, culture, personal goals, trainings, volunteering, travels, conversations, health, humour, hang outs, artistry, fellowship, in fact in all things– glorify you God? Not to place us in a conscious burden of accountability and constant advocacy for all, but knowing if it helps another to discover Christ through our living, even though we are yet still making a progressive growth in Christ, then to this generation we owe the gospel.

xli. You cannot afford to play down the gifts of the spirit or ignore exercising its fruit– a necessary synergy. These, the spiritual keys, the reason of the manifestation of the grace of God. Quench not the spirit but work in alliance with Him, maximally. <u>The spiritual leader has to think gifts and fruit[s] (fruit of the spirit, fruit in righteousness)</u>. It's a mockery to the grace of God to think that the spirit who supplies the grace to show or bear the fruit cannot supply the grace to function according to His spirit and enable the gifts to be operational. Some think they made the fruit active, that is impossible; that will be forced character, acting, behaviour modification, false fruit. God has to lead through us to operate in the fullness of the fruit of the Spirit and His gifts. Individuals may be deceived but never God cannot be mocked. Ananias and Sapphire thought their kindness should be affirmed by the Church but the Spirit of God showed the Apostles they were bragging about their gift and had hid some, misrepresenting the size and quality of it, wanting the praise as people of character, but God saw through. Shockingly He killed them. And godly fear came on all around. Do we speak of the Simon in Samaria in the bible, who wanted to buy the spiritual gift of the spirit, showing disregard for the Spirit and exercising no godly fruit. God was displeased with his attitude, and the attempt to make merchandise of the grace of God. Apostle Peter rebuked him. Often those who play down the work and gift of the spirit never really have any, nor fruit of the spirit either, even if they claim to. Nonetheless, if God has blessed you, be mindful of your gift and never fail to give glory to God and let him continue to work on you as you bless all others. You will need both as a leader, your gift and fruit.

xlii. Through trials and persecution God will grow the leader. The spiritual leader understands that, and is patient through the trial if it comes. God does not tempt any with evil, but allows it, as a sovereign God, because He knows He is in control and also will not allow you to take on more than you can handle [*James 1:13; 1 Corinthians 10:13*]. One can say He allows it because of the scripture which tells us that. A spiritual leader would understand that and be patient in tribulation, rather than take options that are unhelpful and not glorifying to God. Leadership requires you lead those God put in your trust with this understanding lest they murmur against the Lord. Life sometimes test you, and some have wondered, God where are you? Yet to be mature is to hold yourself together. Satan is powerless before God who made him, even though through his schemes we are often targeted and subjected to pressures. To stand firm, you will need to know God is all powerful and actually leads your battle and is in front of you in your decision making, that He is absolutely in control, and a sustainer. When Satan planned the death of Christ, he caused a group to arise against the Lord chanting crucify Him, he entered the heart of His disciple Judas Iscariot to sell the Lord out and make others afraid, that they denied Him and fled. He thought he has brought evil across the camp of the Lord and against Him, but God allowed this to happen, and had been aware even Satan came to existence, that it was through the suffering of Christ salvation and redemption will come to mankind, after Adam fell. Satan is responsible for his ill, some of the disciples were as well, and those who participated negatively– but none was to escape the evil consequences of sin and the judgement; yet the priviledge of forgiveness in Christ is reserved for humanity. Satan cannot retrace his steps and will face his judgement at the end of age when God judges the world, but it is given to the human race to seek God and escape that. <u>God planned that through the temptations, persecution, suffering and death of the Lord, that hearts will be tested, His</u>

purpose accomplished, and Christ's glory gained. Even so is our story who trust Christ, that God is faithful to gauge our maturity and accordingly not let the enemy of our soul attack us to destroy our confidence in God, more then we can take on, but when any challenge comes we know before that moment God had already enabled us to stand for Him. God can make everything work for good, so much so Satan wished the attack didn't begin. But as one mature in faith and spiritual you already have a sense that God is in control, and when all the craziness around all ends it will be for a testimony.

xliii. Spiritual leaders are mindful of seven keys for a vibrant relationship. This came to me by revelation. Just before a night rest, the spirit of God stirred me to pick up my pen and write. Some I knew before by His word, but He reminded me and coordinated all in my memory. I saw arcs as lines, lopped over each other, as though creating vibrating sounds upwards. And as ripples of water moving northwards. It was a sense of God speaking to my heart on breaking through seven specific layers of veils that could limit a relationship. Quite briefly I would highlight them, as we trust the spirit to minister to our hearts, even more in specifics, and bring stillness only the Holy Spirit can bring. These are healthy tips and options:

1. The willingness to be vulnerable and to share past experiences together with those spiritually mature and trusting God to heal you from everything that troubles your heart, as you talk to each person [*Malachi 3:16; James 5:16*].

2. Having your foundation on God, and shared faith interest in Christ, as revealed in the word of God (Bible) [*Matthew 22:29; Ephesians 5:19*].

3. Develop intimacy intentionally. Where married do not neglect being together emotionally and sexually [*1 Corinthians 7:5; Songs of Solomon 8:7; Ecclesiastics 9:9*].

4. Communication is also so vital. Let your yes be yes, and no, no. As Jesus advised. He wasn't suggesting inflexibility or lack of compassion, but rather sincerity. Of the need to avoid words that cause misunderstanding, verbal reprisal attacks, but building each other spiritually with care [*1Corinthians 15:33; Matthew 5:37; James 3:10; Jeremiah 17:9*].

5. Trust God for steps in godly influences around you, your family, friends and partnerships. The right influence will inspire you to good works [*Proverbs 18:24*].

6. Singularity of vision is core, else divided and conflicting interests will not take you farther in purpose [*Amos 3:3; Psalm 133:1; John 6:68*].

7. Sacrificial love is necessary, a blessed gift. Whether at a personal, financial, cultural, forgiving level etc In the world most things are paid for in return for transaction to occur, Christ rather has borne the cost of whatever price we were supposed to pay, and has given us spiritual freedom and elevation [*John 15:13*].

xliv. Spiritual leaders are able to receive and interpret revelatory visions, pictures, moments, seasons, and dream. They are able to discern which dream is of the devil, or a product of weariness and excess of food, and that which is of God [that is of divine guidance and vision of the night; *Ecclesiastics 5:3, Genesis 31:11*]. They are able to discern a God-moment, an occurrence out of the norm pointing to the divine, a divine visitation, a spiritual sign with sensitivity to what God is saying or of strangeness in the heavens yet holding some wisdom (as with the wise men who discern that sighting had more than the illumination of darkness) [*1 Chronicles 12:32; Genesis 18:2; Hebrews 13:2; Luke 19:44; John 13:20*], also they are able to recognise other gifted and spiritual people like them and leap in their spirit with excitement rather than rivalry. Visionaries are only visionaries because they have seen a vision, and not just a vision, a God-inspired vision. <u>We are rewarded not for what we make happen, but how we hear the heart of God</u> and walk in step with that. I hope you can grasp this. The world can conjure or replicate a vision and execute it, as you often see in friendship clubs and organisations, often seeking to erase any spiritual input or link to God, just as one could eat without considering God's input but yet should. Christian ministry is however, rather letting God have His way, His vision, as much as those in the generation hears, to transform lives for His glory, then these other structures become an addendum to the main meat for which it was made, in the time frame He permits.

xlv.   <u>You cannot be a spiritual leader commanding spiritual influence in the territory where you are placed unless you understand how to pray in all dimensions</u> [*Matthew 6:5-18; Ephesians 6:18; Luke 18:1*]. In James 5:16, we see that it is the prayer of the righteous that moves God. Understanding how to pray is key. There is the prayer of thanksgiving, intercession, making of requests before God, declaration of the intent of heaven on earth by scriptures and spiritual understanding, praying in the spirit, a prayer of authority exercised over the powers of darkness casting them out. There all forms of prayer, so it is vital to understand how to pray in all manners available. There is a kind of communication with the divine that is not borne out of a need, but of adoration. A thankfulness for life, the breathe, for nature– creation, for the gift of humanity and friendship, for the potentials that are possible by being alive, that despite challenges that are often so real, and evil which ever seems so near, that there are treasures hidden, in often overlooked places, that we have to refocus and harness to birth or bring out. Thanks, also for the gifts that come our way, either through work or favour– that which God brings. As a leader do you know of intercession? For Kings in the bible times needed this, as some leaders in this present time may realise they need, to seek the guidance of the divine from priests and godly men; seeking their advice and counsel. As a spiritual leader it is your responsibility however to always pray for them– whether they ask for or not. Intercession is to stand for their sake and the people they govern, so everyone may have peace, until the will of God is established. This is not out of place if we want to harness the blessing of the greater power from God, rather than to seek magicians, sorcerers, horoscopes. Intercession is making a spiritual case on behalf of someone before God– how, so much we all need this. People who care enough to pray for us. Not that God may just hear us, but that He may hear and answer, and glorify His name. If only the righteous by the grace of God, in everyplace prayed more often concerning a situation, it will send a spiritual signal to heaven of the necessity of that situation more. Consider, God not being unjust, He will hear. Whilst God could intervene in a situation to bring justice and exercise His discretionary rule, there are specific times He will act in direct and specific response to prayer. What intercession does, is, seek the mercy of God for another who may be operating in full blown ignorance, asking God for mercy and time for them to come to their senses, for delayed judgement, for reconciliation to God, for those under their influence to not be affected, for communities to be blessed. Often, they become more effective when redeemed, and even more thankful, perhaps later, that God was patient and didn't destroy a person, a nation in their wickedness immediately. There will be those who despite repeated warnings fail to honour God– prayers could also be one of those mechanisms to make a spiritual request concerning their reign to be stopped, or that the full purpose concerning the situation be exercised according to His discretion. Few believers understand they can resist the devil and declare he leaves, whilst conferring and declaring the purpose of God stand. This I will expatiate more before the brethren, however, it is sufficient for you to know answered prayers are proof of spiritual leaders, as their prayers make things happen in the spirit, and in God's time. I will urge you to never become complacent to prayer. Man listens, God listens, even technology listens, but it is God that hears and answers prayer. Enough said. False miracle could be faked and some may contrive coincidences to obfuscate the relevance of the divine, or to attempt to hide it until there is 'empirical evidence' to revise and explain what just happened, just as making parody of an original composition, but make no mistake there still exists unique God-moments and intervention where it is obvious and undeniable there has been the miraculous and supernatural, where empirical evidence may even show an external effect than human intervention, in comparison to operations in natural parameters. In essence, where evidence show whatever happened is out the natural order, one has to inquire what has caused it. It will take someone spiritually perceptive to draw a spiritual diagnosis. This explains why Christ shook the world, rising from the dead after days buried, raising the dead many times, and the other miracles He did which were clearly out of the norm, these raised questions and made even clearer pointers to the affirmation of that which is superior– God, working with Him and in Him. It is good to know God is in control and makes all things work for good to those who fear and trust Him.

xlvi. Effective management of task is necessary in leadership. That may require spacing out your work, or delegation to get more done. This would require the right place and time, but also maturity. This is also a spiritual principle. Thousands of years ago, Moses's father in law Jethro, would advise his son-in-law, to delegate his work and prioritise only the hard cases, giving more room to rest so he doesn't breakdown from a spiritual work [*Exodus 18:17-27*, also Christ would break His task into smaller sizes, He formed mini-groups to feed the multitudes *Luke 9:14*. Two principles here, breaking into smaller bits and also delegating, that is encouraging others to take on some of the work]. Achieving numbers is not as important as gaining competences or reaching effectiveness, as people of faith. When their faith and obedience qualifies them, then any building on, by obedience, such as training is possible. Also, effective management is gathering the fragment to avoid wastage. But my focus is the ability to re-concentrate, refocus, calibrate efforts to reach people. In Jethro and Jesus's scenario, queues will be shorter and needs reached quickly, as responsibility was taken to serve the people in smaller sized up structures, and more hands brought in for administration. Think of how this may apply to today's practical situations– where say you as the Chief Operation Manager for a relief organisation working in conflict areas, and you need to administer support service and engage with the community in the interim whilst efforts are ongoing for a lasting solution (if your job description is adjusted to this). You will need as much support as you can get apart from the resources available for distribution, in volunteers and employed staff, rather than doing it yourself. You will also have to breakdown your work into daily tasks, and not try to fit a lot into a day than you can manage. Hardly do we acknowledge God for principles as these, tested for thousands of years before. Its like a child who receives fund from the parents and says what is needed is the money not them. To argue that God is not needed for everyday practicalities is to not consider the source, the beginning. Or to say you don't need to be spiritual to think of these principles, its like the child saying the parents' faces should be on the currency to prove ownership of the fund, or that they gave it. Some have applied God's wisdom without reference to Him, but the ideal and better way is to receive God and His wisdom. Best put, the one who created us and gave us the ability to even think, differently and similarly in some ways. Furthermore, one must ask how to do a task that not only minimises waste of time but of energy. A leader must consider that good organisation avoids depletion of strength. I share a personal story for your guidance. In early 2017 I perceived there was the need to teach on faith and focus my thoughts mainly on this as it pertains to the Lord Jesus Christ. On how through Christ (meaning the anointed one, messiah) faith in God is possible and what that portends– the scripture was to be my guide. Also, I knew this would fill minds with the word of God and help against often distractions in a frivolous news prone world, and also bless those who hear. To achieve this, it was important to spread the task; so I did set out to consistently share my thoughts on some of my online platforms and meditate on this— specifically between 8am-9am, Sunday to Friday, whilst Saturday was to be a rest day. This was throughout the year, beginning from the first day to the last. The biblical based messages were not automated nor was a personal assistant employed, I had to get it done myself but saw the need to spread the effort out through the week than take a long stretch in a day, giving room to do other things afterwards, and encouraged others who received it to then share with their friends. I noticed often it required preparing before, sometimes the night before, in other cases in the morning. However, the joy was to have the word of God minister and bobbling in one's heart. I also noticed the word truly is strength for the heart, of those who trust Christ. There are Christian devotionals that also provide daily spiritual meat for readers, and often challenge people to follow through a 365 days commitment. This is a powerful example as people are taught to make spiritual meditation a lifestyle and to understand they can learn much by making short daily commitments. Again, in reference to Jesus' case when He fed the crowd after asking them to sit in smaller group, the disciples were able to share in that specific time, and witness the far-reaching ability of God to multiply their meals, and to help create positive habits. Aligning yourself with wisely built structures and managing tasks efficiently will not diminish the miraculous in anyway. For me, towards the end of the year I realised I wasn't just being reactive but rather the word of God was shaping my day and thoughts, which is great. It was comforting me and I became a timely instrument of comfort as well, and providing biblical teaching support to others too. I would hope many gained from it; and fragments of the teachings are now also available on some of the books I authored. One main lesson I gained is you could achieve more by being efficient. It would seem I was always online, but in reality I understood some may spend more time focusing on junk information for hours and sharing same, with energy that could have been saved for more productive work, or choose to spread their efforts over the week. The zeal of the lord must lead us to share our faith not only online but on the streets, at work when opportunities arise in especially in forms of questions in our spare time, and in any place as necessary. I was encouraging some friends in the gospel in a meeting as we sat round a table sometime ago, I recall saying to them, don't bother about a burnout if you are not burning. You must make sure if another believer relapsed into your kind of spiritual state they would not be accused of a burnout because you are so docile and inefficient for the kingdom of God; we ought to able to inspire and live out our lives for Christ, and continue on the work we are called to do! Even if that means getting more hands on, or spreading out the tasks so you can manage complex assignments. Allow God to lead you per time, but keep your spiritual fire lit, so you can be warm, and others can see and be warm as well.

xlvii. Some heart to leadership means not being heavy-handed but temperate in all things. Consider Rehoboam in the old testament [*1 King 12*], his response to the elders who requested he lessen their burdens. His refusal brought about a divided kingdom, the loyalty to the house of King David was compromised. All because of a brute and insensitive decision.

Taking responsibility is recognising your actions impact on others. Of course, 'others' who have to be also individually responsible on their own score. <u>Sometimes strength is lessening burdens, not because you have no authority to increase same but because you have wisdom to empathise with the weak and the stressed amongst you.</u> I must reiterate, the one who considers the poor, feeble or disadvantaged is blessed by the almighty God, and their profiting will be evident to all. Scriptures talks about the meek inheriting the earth. Why be heavy handed, when you can choose the way of compassion? Does it make you look weak? Would you rather be feared than loved with reverential fear?

xlviii. Spiritual leaders are sensitive but smart. They could either get worked up with 'How could you say that' or rather choose to say, 'This is what I would say and do to make the situation better.' Often, they chose the latter, meaning to use less energy than to cause strain, but deciding to be more productive. It is to use one's 'breath' and communication to lay out concrete plans which is more durable, and which puts you technically-up in the end, rather than dwell on frivolities. You need not be perturbed if criticism of you suggest incompetence– where true, it may benefit you to improve, where barefacedly untrue, you would make sure you ascertain if it is such to cause distraction and ridicule you so you don't benefit from the gains of your work out of malice, then ignore it, except you deem it sufficient because of a possible damage to refute it considerably. I think more needful than not, is not to dwell on frivolities. I notice some persons could enjoy talking complete junk and in a toxic manner, if I can well describe it, or speak in a way that intentionally do not make sense, in a way that hides information and fails to appeal to basic logic. This do occur. If someone says he is poor and cannot afford food, the response is hardly why are you hungry, except you are aiming for some higher truth– some sense will be to connect the dots, that if he is poor and cannot afford food, it would substantially explain the hunger situation. Except you are bordering on insensitivity or a desire to deliberately annoy, you start rubbing sores, with directly snobbish questions, with a desire to get a targeted feedback. I would suggest a spirit-styled leader would be drawn to soothing hearts and navigating conversations to speak truth tactfully were necessary but not to tear people apart and leave lives ruined.

What excitement would be in that? I concede it requires some level of intelligence to construct some mind-boggling sentences, and to possess some level of wit– it may help you navigate some murky waters in conversations, or some persons who are intentionally out to fish for your personal data without wanting to have a humanly relationship but to trade knowledge of you to your damage or for gossip. To such being mute or ignoring might help, except you have a prompt in your spirit to do otherwise. There are leaders in political offices who may conserve the facts for purposes of security, but the goal should be, not leading people astray on false premises. Not every stranger deserves to know your street; and where someone has stolen any of your vital and personal information, breaching your privacy, such a person or sponsoring organisation have not done well, and needs to make amends.   Christ would not divulge anything to Herold, but to Pilate He would briefly disclose who He was [*John 19; Luke 23:6-12*]. The intention behind this is not spelt to us in the scriptures, but Christ had fore-taught the need to be wise as a serpent but harmless as a dove [*Matthew 10:16*], not only to escape ill treatment but more to stay in the father's will. To His disciples, those close to Him, His inner caucus, He spoke deeply, but to the crowd more in parables, less plainly, but the interpretations more to His disciples [*Matthew 13:34; Mark 4:34*]. And this is the Lord's attitude? Incredibly, positive. I wonder how we then should live, perhaps with much more care than we presently do? I think we can start now to begin to be much more circumspect, because of those out to find out what we think, with no intention to apply the truth. Because of those looking for showmen, but with no real interest in what Christ offers. Sometimes it is too much for some to bear, and we need a veil, a parable, a rhetoric– they may need a longer time to digest the meaning; and may need someone to ask what the quoted scriptures mean. Will the truth of the bible benefit you if your desire is not to learn honestly, to probe further to satisfy the soul, but to find occasion for ridicule of the message and the messenger? Wise Bible teachers would suggest the need to avoid unnecessary arguments. I personally think it gives needless headaches, nothing compared to Christ's disciples who got maltreated for being too persuasive or winning an argument, such that it caused rebellion [*Acts 14*]. You must inquire if that's an approach the Spirit of God wants you to take, to debate a point- I think it the talk is not engaging or any being receptive there is really no need to go on, as it would not profit the hearers. God doesn't strive with man's heart forever, He never compels any forcefully. There may be need for reasoned argument where the hearer is willing to communicate as well. Although the gospel is offensive it only ministers to those open-hearted. It must be ministered to the saving of the soul; but allow the Spirit to show you the right words, time, and when to let go and let God speak Himself. I always wonder when someone keeps insisting to hear your view, almost as proof you talk, saying get in the game, but the problem is some people get offended if it doesn't go their way, and start acting outside the rules– to insult and make other vices. The best is to avoid such. Consider Paul's advice to Timothy– to avoid vain babblings [*Titus 3:9; 2 Timothy 2:23*], it helps. <u>As a spiritual leader the calling requires being smart but sensitive. You wouldn't let the voice of the poor or marginalised be silenced, sometimes it has to go past you to others' concern and needs.</u> Sometimes truth is difficult to say but needs to be heard, but, love in speech is good. We ought to consider those who need help, especially when its in your power to do so, individually or as a society. Often it is said believe in yourself, that is true, also consider the power of team, of formidable structures, and inclusion, you will benefit from your strength but from the wisdom and affirmation of others around you. Helping others through wise counsel is crucial and a very practical way to lifts heart. Also, in addition to working alongside teams, the same principle of sensitivity and being wise applies, you don't want your presence to be suffocating but indispensable, a hard balance to strike though, but also consider how by the help of the spirit of God your individual gifting is not obliterated, nor the team's uniqueness lost. Consider building each other, enhancing each's objectives. There cannot be a deliberate policy to make a group or person less positively productive or inconsequential, or to exacerbate fear, or to influence negative action. Each person must take responsibility for their decisions, so must leadership equally bear responsibility when decisions are not blessing the weakest, or depletes the strength of the advantaged for no helpful reason– how about raising each to par. The leader considers ways to make the weak strong and keep the strong strong. I don't think this has to always conflict. Scripture speaks of the

Exodus journey, there was none feeble amongst them [*Psalm 105:37*]. There was grace of God released supernaturally to make all strong. The early Church leaders and Christ's disciples considered it an error to have division in the Church, between two groups, the Hebrews and Hellenist [those of the diaspora], fellow brothers and sisters in the Christian faith, as the food wasn't distributed evenly, quickly the Apostles who were also resident at this time in Jerusalem as overseers acted to ensure this integral ministry was given the necessary impetus and focus it deserved by appointing spiritual leaders to give central thought to it– the leaders where men of faith, full of the Holy Spirit, but also of proven reputation, able to serve the people [*Acts 6:1-7*]. Imagine a family, or nation that decides to make all strong- to adopt a bare minimum that lifts standard to an enviable proportion, whether be educationally, health-wise, life expectancy, matters of morality and social justice, in created opportunities, shelter arrangements, care for dependents. This would not mean limiting others' entrepreneurial drive or curtailing their growth and capital investments, but creating an atmosphere where the minimum standards adopted makes the future attractive for those willing to work. This way everyone gains, and the whole land prospers. It is possible to see the wellbeing of each other in a community as crucial. Though some think of the risk of a few who may prefer to supress others as soon as they get to a fortunate position, perhaps on some good evidence others too may do the same should they have an advantage– then the circle of fear continues. A bridge that supports structures that lifts people up, who in turn make a commitment to lift others, will break negative stereotypes, this comes by deliberate inclusion and taking the initiative to pursue and work towards harmonisation. I will like to think there is some plausible explanations for gaps in development across a spectrum, where there is lack of shared experiences and innovation, even though these solutions have arisen both through personal discoveries or the effort of think-tank teams from a range of sectors. Those who are able to benefit from the spread or even merchandise of it, would be those who become part of an acclaimed community in history and are not trapped from the collective progresses made, and able to more fully articulate their stance and recover from any general established pattern of relinquished resource brought about by conflict. A spiritual leader understands the need to bridge the divide, consider objectively inherent deficiencies internally and at grassroot level, and have goals in unison as a team, group, community, or nation, to be propelled on a constant forward trajectory. This is what I'm saying. The step begins from you, anyone reading this– by changing your mentality. Rather than focusing on flaws, which is often a product of living in a spiritually fallen world– and the associated weakness often evenly spread but yet with great richness in it, how about considering the potential for doing more great things through working smartly together with others in your community or street where you at, or perhaps nation, to birth a vision that will impart lives positively long term. And to consider building godly systems, rather than always being reactive or critical, or thriving in a maze without an exit and without knowledge of what exists in the open area; not as though there is anything wrong in good functional space, but it has to be such endorse-able and born from goodwill. The idea is how we can bring godly wisdom, love, blessing in to situations and sustain structures of empowerment– surely it is a good thing. God delights in godly reasoning, and you knowing

He wills you flourish. On the other hand, it seems there are those in the world who thrives on creating abhorrent disparities. True. And it is the case that less opportunities for some have always existed, often side by side with stupendous wealth, and in varied contexts, yet our response is not to do nothing, but to take steps to support the weak amongst you. As sin is present in our world, so the need for the transforming power of the gospel of salvation, that brings righteousness and sanctification, needs to be present and activated. God assures us, a day is coming when all brokenness in the world will be fixed, in complete perfection, materially and spiritually, all round.

xlix. Spiritual leaders understand the part sanctifies the whole, and they connect with this principle to benefit spiritually. It's like a yeast affecting the whole lump, in the making of a dough. It's the first fruit of the harvest honouring God. It's the tithe set apart from your produce and profit for the providing of the needs at God's temple and for His servants. The part in question may seem insignificant but if dedicated to the purpose designed for it, it makes the whole worthwhile. It's the early years of grace, mercy and love, that nurtures the life span of that that is precious.

The enemy of our soul battles us at this time; yet we see from Jesus' early years that there was conniving to snuff his life at this time, but God wouldn't allow it, as His purpose wasn't established yet. Moses was threatened so he couldn't be a deliverer whilst he sojourned in Egypt, but God saved him. Also, I perceive you may be under attack because you desire to birth your dreams in faith, but you must pray and persevere. One could intercede for another— by not imputing faults, by loving and being lovable, by allowing the Holy Spirit in you work through every part of your life, horning your skills for God's glory. The Church must also receive the blessing of the part, so it can be fully nourished as a whole, that may be people from several parts of the world, with varied talents, with different cultures, looking peculiarly, sounding unique in speech, talking many languages, with different character traits and temperament— yet God has designed it this way, that by benefiting from each other we grow the body [*Ephesians 4:15-16; 1 Corinthians 12:12-27*]. The wonders of the little things, as the tongue, it is that which controls the whole body. The tongue is a little member as Apostle James says, it yet controls the mighty [*James 3; Proverbs 18:21*]. And I dare say it shapes nations and the destiny of many and must be used wisely. If in error vain words are spoken, by deliberate action speak better words to move and create your future positively. Words are action. Words are life. The right one will help you, not mar you, it would make you good for action.

1. <u>There is need to see that where there is authority, the one under authority need to be comfortable being under one.</u> Also refuse the fears of any entrenched 'paternalistic complexity' as though ~~certain roles are gender defined only and always, or~~ staying away from responsibility because of fear. Also, be sure that where responsibility has been bestowed on you by God he equally supplies the grace to live up to it– only be in alignment to His spirit. To be in spiritual authority over others do not absolve you from also being under authority– first under God to whom you're also accountable, but also to those who by the grace of God are more mature than you. To them you owe a responsibility to also listen and to honour God in your actions. Be careful to think you must listen to no one, or that the scriptures are outdated and no longer speaks in the 21st century, or for going forward. The scripture addresses the sin problem in man and reveals God's plan for the now and future. It would be a heathenistic mistake to ignore the living word of God, as revealed in Christ– and to ignore the teachings of the written word documented for our

learning. There, we see the power of God in creation by his spoken word– as God's power is without limit. Can't the one who created blind eyes with the mud, also speak to blind eyes to open? Well Jesus Christ did, and can. Can't the one who made the heavens and the earth also provide wisdom to man to take care of it? I believe God can. I urge us then not to rebel against His word, but rather come under divine authority.

li.   <u>Leaders willing to read and gain valuable information [through varied methods accessible] are only the ones that will be educated and able to educate others. Same in relation to the dynamics of spiritual leadership. Do you understand, and are properly educated on spiritual matters?</u> Can you bring leadership in this niche area and illustrate how it is essential to practical living? Spiritual leaders understand the need to gain the necessary spiritual repertoire through diligent study [*2 Timothy 2:15*]. First, because they will be equipped to handle life's pressures with apt skills and knowledge gained, and because they have the wisdom to know they need much intellectual help from the great resource base available in the world today from people of repute– utilising the ability to choose the right knowledge to learn even greater practical spiritual principles and relevant secular skills. In the word, Hebrews 13:20-21; Ephesians 4:11-16, we see in the equipping of the saints, it is God actually working to enable effectiveness. <u>God equips us, so we can equip others. Through the study of the word of God, and also with the help of mature believers we come to understand the mind of God and then are able to communicate same to others priviledged to hear</u>. For this reason, God has raised officers in the body of Christ able to present the truth they have received through spiritual insight. Only those who have eyes and who see, can impart the revelation of sight. So it is in spiritual matters.

lii. <u>Spiritual leaders learn to understand and know the audience to which they are called to</u>. First to know it is important, and then trust the Lord to help you understand the group. Above all, be prepared to minster to each according to their God given capacity, this means adopting different educational strategies to suit each specific group within the audience. Not everyone is a Professor or unskilled worker, also not everyone is spiritually mature nor everyone immature similarly. To kids, wives, men, brothers, sisters, professionals in the workplace, business people, political actors and so on, all represents specific groups to be reached uniquely, but also one that could have a binding thread of humanity focus running through. The thought is how can I bring a word that appeals to, comforts all in their respective area of need, even a message to a particular culture that is relevant to their needs, and that they understand. Apostle Paul reasoned about this, and was mindful of fulfilling his task and not dissipating his effort [*1 Corinthians 9:16-23; Galatians 2:2; John 12:42-50, 3:17, 9:4; Luke 9:26, 19:13*]. Christ would focus majorly His teachings to the Jews as Abraham's offspring, from the child of promise– Isaac, born of Sarah– his legitimate wife, but yet knew and commissioned His disciples to reach out beyond the borders of Jerusalem to all nations [*John 4:22; Matthew 15:21-28; 8:1-13; 28:18-19*]. Even the Gentiles, those who have no connection whatsoever in the flesh to the promise of Abraham, do share in this heritage by Christ's work- to this group there is also a God-word of hope. The grieving or emotionally stable need the same God, but a word that applies to their needs. The comfort from the spirit in some cases is what He says to one, yet could benefit all hearing. Also, the Lord may have various words for each situation or people, as to the Churches instructed in the book of Revelation. Yet it is the same God at work to the profiting of all. Per time, working with God requires sensitivity and openness to hear where He is leading to and what He is saying. Clearly.

liii.   It takes a spiritual leader to consider that as a people you must consider training to win by faith, and to love always– both elements are intertwined. By faith they show they rely on Christ's work, by love they make their work effective and honourable. To give one's life for a cause by the strength which faith supplies but not love the people you are sent to, is mere routine– they may not know but there is great reward from God who searches the heart. When they find out they were just tools and booty-traps they question even the faith they found. Also, <u>if one gives great love and there is no knowledge which forms the basis of true faith or believing then how sound is such a love?</u> Would it lead to truth or conversion? Is it a love that permits evil? Then that is no love. Godly love is agape– divine, it calls to righteousness, it upholds just causes. It despises a false balance. Yet this love comforts and illuminates faith. Our faith in God actually opens the door for the love of God to flow through us. The one who really has the God kind of faith, if they allow the work of the spirit, they will ooze out great love. A leader wins that allows love to reign, everyone wins, as peace also reigns. You can love when you have faith. You can trust that God is working in a wonderful way to produce love in you towards others, and also not to self-hate.

liv. <u>Spiritual leaders are not agnostic to the creative power of God</u>. God is spirit. The concept of whole connection to the spiritual being that holds all of existence, is the essence of spirituality. Explains why to be a spiritual leader has to do with spirituality in itself, and that, authentic, not feigned as a behavioural contraption of some sort, or human engineered artistry or play. Genesis 5:1-2 shows us humans were made to portray God. Great leaders think about this and decide to live out as such. To fall below God's standard in anything is to live less than is intended for His glory (Ephesians 5:9-14). It is about not letting anything have a hold on you, such that you deny God's power, or rely on any other good thing apart from God. Brethren, Ladies and Gents, you cannot sit on the fence but give the credit due, taking cognisance of His great power. Not because He needs your compliment, but because it reflects your level of understanding and spirituality. I would think a higher understanding would hope in God. And on whether you are set out to lead? Leaders are not experts in all things, but there is an expectation of reasonable proficiency and getting the basic foundations right. It must be such on this side that they have gained sufficient mastery, and I do not think this excludes understanding God's role in setting the course of human nature. This is so they can lead others effectively, with a genuine moral compass though some seem to think its now extinct or irrelevant, and also so one can build on credible wisdom. Christ is the rock in these things, the very fountain of wisdom.

lv.   1 Timothy 4:8 reminds us of maintaining a balanced perspective of the spiritual and physical, also of the promise we have received now but which is to be fulfilled. This is so we don't fall into error or obsession, longing for that which is invisible and spiritual, to the discountenancing of the physical world, or clinging so deeply to the seen that we forget what holds all together exists in a higher plane. How do you as a leader lead an organisation, or people with this kind of mindset? It is acknowledging there needs to be balance between spirit and matter. Basically saying– 'I have seen to my and their spiritual needs, but how can I now fill their stomachs, or encourage some vitality in them through exercise?' Or considering, in this manner– 'As a believer I thank God for saving faith, but I trust God's redemption to come in the consummation of all things– so where the Lord is I will be with Him and stay with Him at all times.' There is no fear in being alive with God's comfort now, or being absent from the physical body but present with the Lord. Neither option is horrifying. Both, is a joy, whether here or there, it is being with the Lord that matters. The tragedy will be existence without God. Neither is there ignorance that a willingness to make a prayer for health is not at variance with a good pattern of bodily care or treatment when due, as the same God supplies the herbs and creative sense to humanity to treat, with layers of developing knowledge passed down through the generations. <u>That balance of the functionality of spirit and the physical world, brings sense to our relational engagement</u>. We can find restraint because we know of a God who is active today. We can take responsibility because we know God has empowered us to make certain decisions ourselves. We can worship God because we understand the limits in our rationality, our proficiency– that all could end, that yes, we have some control but not 100%. There is a God who authors the balance.

lvi. <u>As a leader it would send the wrong message and make a mess of good ethics if you make excuses for wickedness you see, even if you are not directly involved– there is great wisdom in not recommending it.</u> Consider Proverbs 11:1. Why tilt the balance to deceive those that can't decipher? And hope if they do, they better play along or be reprimanded for standing against evil? What if the definition of evil is not so complicated to know, as apparent to the discerning, and that all is not perfect in the world does not excuse certain grievous actions or make as one for a guise. You don't say because none is good by any standard, so let's maim the vulnerable. 'Like, seriously?' Leadership then, spiritual leadership, is drawing a line, understanding that our humanity calls us to some basic rational norms, of love and mutual respect. And perhaps, if one cannot be at the forefront in pushing for these values, then at least avoid disrupting the practice of such from the side-lines. It would seem fair we all embrace what is good for us and our fellowman. It is like avoiding moving the goal post to dodge the opponent's goal, or constantly adjusting the rules to embarrass, rather than laying solid basis for overall actions, that would be weird. At some point it would be ludicrous to gainsay wisdom when you see it. There is no justification for evil because of suffering or the presumption of one, as though those who in a godly manner frown at evil have no right to because they are not in that situation themselves. What situation exactly to precipitate a vain response? How does evil become a conscious option? I would think rather than anchor on evil, the option is to repent and consider those affected. Rarely do anyone have a monopoly of doing evil, often all of humanity is plagued with the temptation to deviate, but the restraint of righteousness must be constantly appealing. The spiritual person understands the benefits at the end of a righteous walk is usually good. I think also that to endorse a wrong course of action or evil, and at the same time be saying, let's see how miracles are wrought to make things right. It's like an employer dismissing an employee for no cause and saying, let's see how you pray yourself back to this job. Well, there is a couple of alternatives for God if He needs to sort things, possibly including exchanging positions or granting new opportunities. But I would like to think God would not sweat to prove Himself as competently in control behind the scenes, or rise up to the challenge of a particular employer perched somewhere in the globe when he calls, reactively. He will when He knows it is time. There is the pride in always wanting to be calling the shots, deciding who answers to you, but you see God is not human, and would come when it's time– Christ would go see Lazarus when it was time. Few days late, but didn't stop the miraculous from happening– his resurrection from the dead by the power of Christ [*John 11*]. God help us, wait for Him, and not offer our sacrifice before it is time, and committing a great evil of discountenancing the Lord's will and pattern. In essence, the miracle is the empowerment to do right because not everyone has that desire, it takes the supply of God's spirit [*Genesis 39:9*]. To suppress the will and strength of the spirit and to instruct God against His purpose, is to tempt, and mock His power. If He moves, yet still many may still find occasion to doubt, and another excuse. Except by mercy. More often than not God will not be cajoled by people's opinion, or intimidated– like in the Rich man and Lazarus story [*Luke 16:19-31*]. He most likely would insist there are others who will be His instrument for good or evil– rarely is God dependent on one alone [*Hebrews 12:9, Isaiah 45:7*]. Furthermore, on not excusing wickedness, consider this– if one knows needless lies is being perpetrated to cause fear then the propaganda should lose its potency over you, because you know the truth of the agenda and aim. To accept the fear do not serve you right, nor a just cause. Also, to say, I can encourage violence because those affected are not bothered themselves will be a preposterous scenario. Or where in turn, neglecting or abusing an individual or group is acceptable because culture or an organisation accepts it, and promotes such as permissible adverts for the next generation, that too will be heart wrenching. Instead, to shield, and come alongside others in need will be a good thing. And to create a solid understanding of pursuing righteousness in the fear of God will be commendable. Better still to not hack down the future aspirations of those who one leads as a spiritual leader, or to allow for flames of conflict to be fanned. These pangs of evil do not bring upliftment and are such to resist in Christ's name.

lvii. A leader that is a genuine visionary must be 'open' to make provision for needs, as 'provision.' And because God is the provider of both the provision and vision, there is no need to fret. In Christ's interaction and engagement with Philip, one of His disciples, He used him to see to the needs of those in hunger and distress, He knew it would cost a lot feeding the multitude following Him when He asked for the need to be met [*John 6:5*]. As with Abraham– God provided the needed ram for sacrifice. His name is Jehovah Jireh [the Lord who provides]. He said to Philip, basically, forget the cost in this instance, ask them to sit, and He then proceeded to multiply miraculously the bread and fish, and fed thousands. Why? Consider, how many times some may have had to turn away potential converts, because of the financial cost of training disciples or even meeting the practical needs of those who we minister to, and others we engage with on the streets and other places. Some may say, would you help us with hot meals in your meetings if you invite us, and we go possibly, some other time. Or, some say, I am homeless, and we say, hope you are fine in days. Often because the needs are so enormous to reach every person. Yet Christ calls us to trust He would help meet this need through setting aside what we have got already. Providing a reference to a place of help? How about praying with them and buying a cup of drink or a meal, give a little, or help complete an application? Supporting those we can in anyway possible, for a time? Or a few, even if not all. What is being canvased is what is important, we are not hoarding God's provision– least we find ourselves fighting Christ. Rather, our consideration should be to support those in need, that we can, according to the measure of our resource, no matter how little. Thinking ahead how to tackle a vision, storing up, ahead of time. So when it is time to execute the vision, the step of provision has already been sourced and met. I believe that according to the measure of grace we have received God could multiply much more. If we give him our five or seven, he could reach thousands more. They too could become powerful seeds to reach more in years to come when well off. I perceive God is saying, what do you have in your hands?

lviii. Have you ever thought of love, as that which is owed to another? A debt to pay humanity. <u>It becomes a personal responsibility and more strategic to living a more fulfilling life. Knowing what you are called to love, and those you owe love to is crucial.</u> God's word reminds us that if anyone loves the 'world,' meaning all it represents, the cunning systems of it, brute force, materialism, hate, selfish driven interests and schemes, all manner of sin, then the love of God is clearly not at work in that person. You are called however to love those in the world, the people, not their ways. To love those who hate and use you and seek your hurt, with truth in love, not affirming their wickedness but considering they are but human. To love them with God's manner of love. Loving them is not a free way ticket to accepting all vile practices or condoning their vices. Its not watering down boundaries and discipline but receiving the chastisement of the Lord as necessary. It is following God's pattern of sweet love, which includes chastisement as appropriate, one that does not respect persons. Love is not giving what someone is not entitled to. This is mature love. For those sceptical of my teaching, I will break it down to your understanding. Love is giving your sexual priviledges to someone you are committed to in a marriage context. A biblical pattern that is really helpful in building trust. God's word is tested and certain, and often the preferable and best part, it would help you walk in humility and in the godly fear and reverence of Christ. The way of love is God's way. If you want to know God's way this is it, and we find it through Christ's strength and help. Also, it is good to know there is forgiveness in Christ when any backslides into any sin, as sin is not consistent with the life of righteousness the believer of Jesus Christ has been called into. A believer of Christ is called not to just love but as Christ would. To receive Christ is embracing the spiritual life in Christ. To embrace Christ's identity, is to put on Christ. To follow His teaching on love, on life and how to live in a way that has reverence for God Almighty and empathy for others. Christ sets a high standard, by laying His life for us. The call to spiritual leadership is beyond leading others or being a place of spiritual influence alone, but being in step with the Spirit of God in obedience– the humble before God and men is the greatest example for spiritual leadership [*Mark 9:35*]. As 'Christ would' is the driving force of this challenge. Christ though being all powerful yet subject to the elements of nature, and engaging as equals with those He created, living with them, eating with those of His days, and ministering to their needs, not putting up a royal appearance even though He could, but serving, even though Lord of all. Think of that for a minute, would you? How would Christ love a colleague at work? How would Christ deal with taxes? How would Christ deal with a complaint? How would Christ treat a spouse? [though He had none on earth, yet He is the repository of all knowledge so would know] How would Christ treat those who bless Him or those who malign Him? With what manner of zeal would Christ attend to Father God's business? How would Christ reward courage in the face of pressure and adversity? How would Christ react to opinions? How would Christ rebuke those who are contemptible and are disrespectful, especially to God's house? How would Christ treat the weak, abused, sick, oppressed? How would Christ address the repentant and truthfully seeking the truth of God? We often see Christ in scriptures balance justice and love, mercy and truth, and showing His justice with mercy, and love in truth. He recognised He had to pay taxes but also understood God deserved His place and in not oppressing the poor. Christ saw the great and small as the same, worthy of honour. For Christ loving was a duty to our neighbour but also a heart issue, as you expect your reward from God, not the praise of men, and for good works. Christ would show us loving our spouse is God's agenda, as He loves the Church of God by purchasing her by His blood on the cross– as from the beginning of Adam and Eve, the Church then is the bride awaiting the bridegroom. For Christ, forgiveness is what we have to have and must do to another as we too are recipients of God's forgiveness. So how would Christ react and love? He let the condemned by men walk free– both the woman caught in the act and the criminals together at His crucifixion were free, if only they would believe and receive His offer of grace. So was Peter who denied the Lord, and other Apostles who left but would later know the grace of God. So, did Saul a former murderer of a Christian martyr who would become renamed Paul and a Christian himself, and become a minister of the gospel of God's grace to the gentiles after a supernatural revelation of Christ. It seems to me that all who come to Christ He loves with tremendous love. We are all wrapped in His endless love. Sincere trust is based on love and faith, and a progressive testimony of a life being lived in honour of God– and that has to be in the continuous, mutual, in a context of relationship, whether between the divine and humanity, or amongst ourselves as we relate to one another. The gospel is replete of many who found the love of God, by a God whose arms is forever open wide, and He has given all people breath with fresh daily opportunities to know Him whilst alive.

lix.   A leader has to have a humble and thankful heart– as this kind of attitude and knowledge empowers them to receive favour from God. For God fights against the proud, those full of themselves, of their own sense of righteousness or human strength, or better put sense of 'rightness' rather than God's alternative, but He lifts the humble, bestowing them with the grace they need for whatever circumstance they go through. Consider James 4:6 on this principle. Humility towards God is so essential in a spiritual walk. Humility means willingness to listen. A recognition you do not know everything, and that the word of God can increase your learning on faith, on humanity, and impart on our ability to live life to the full, and enhancing all the gift naturally in us and also that which we have come to imbibe, from the progressive contribution of others over the years. Humility is being open to the knowledge of your limitedness. Thankfulness is the gratitude in recognising that that which is external to you fills you, that the divine is the primary source of productive and uncorrupted knowledge. To be humble is to understand God's infinite and complete role in creation, and that includes the creation's productivity in fruitfulness and multiplication, the intertwining benefits, and even the inspiration to humanity to tend and harness the harvest from what is available. Emphasis being, God authored the beginning and end. <u>Humility towards God recognises His sovereignty. Humility towards others recognises the grace of God in them, and their gifts and contributions too– and not to be intimidated by it but be rather thankful for it</u>. There is something special in seeing that as a collective in our world we all make a contribution, some in significantly huge ways others in small but indispensable ways. This however will be distinguished from that which is not a helpful contribution, that level of honesty and acceptance requires humility too.

lx.   A leader needs to grasp that often God takes His children through a journey. Your journey is not my journey, but God is firmly in it navigating your deliverance. Through patience and faith, in time you will be victorious. Obedience however is essential. The children of Israel went from the assurance of God's faithfulness to deliverance from Egypt, to being led through the red sea, to experiencing a continued manifested presence of God for their time in the wilderness, and then were trained by the Spirit of God before coming into their promise knowing that their might and deliverance was from God. Do we not see Christ show us His inception into the world through conception and His patience, and manifestation of the presence of God before His translation into glory? Ought we not to know that the one who called us intend that by faith we be reconciled to God, publicly declare our faith and manifest the glory in this world, and that it is by patience we possess our souls? Those who serve God faithfully in obedience can be able to also share in the spiritual inheritance and the promise of spending eternity with God. For His life in us grants us life with Him. A leader must also understand the strength of His followership and help navigate those led to their best potential with least resistance encountered. The bible says concerning the Exodus journey, God led them by Prophet Moses through a path, so they don't despair because of their enemies and turn back. What a gracious and thoughtful God. One has to love one with such concern. One has to take the initiative to engage relevantly but with much patience, to gauge each's strength and know how to minister to it. What can a person, community, organisation handle? Think good intention plus capacity to receive profitable instruction in leadership. If one needs milk, stuffing meat through a person's mouth does no good, no matter how succulent– then it becomes the ability to understand need and provision. God would lead a nation through a route with less trouble [*Exodus 13:17-18, Deuteronomy 8:2*], as by still non-raging waters [*Psalms 23:2*]– this is God's nature I think, speaking peace and building character. If by any chance He allows the storms to rage, or that the enemy of your soul and peace is able to stir the raging waves or raise an army for violent conflict against you, know that if per chance God allows it, He want an opportunity to rebuke the storm and wants to bring about utmost glory for His name, so many will see and fear the Lord, and give Him praise [*Mark 4:39; Romans 8:28, 31-32*].

lxi. There are those who profit from maligning others– receiving rewards from a dysfunctional situation. The sooner such realise that whatever is the system on which they rely– which rewards that kind of interests irrespective of the clear defectiveness, edging on the potential for profit, forming alliances at the expense of objectivity of the Christian faith which is of the principles of love, empathy, glorifying Christ and on obeying God's instruction; is such to be discarded with, if you want to walk in spiritual leadership. A spiritually led person will seek to honour God, where it requires appreciating what is good in others and not punishing the good to appease the erroneous person. There is a self-activated curse on a person who knows what good is and calls it bad to cause the innocent to suffer and then rejoices in it without repentance, the bible reprimands such. Effective and just structures with a fair balance will readily replace accusations of discrimination, as there will be no basis. Setup principled ways of working that when obviously spelt out it applies to all persons in a manner that helps achieve the goal of treating each person with decency and dignity. Of what use is a meeting or organisation to set one rule for a certain class whether be by financial stratification, gender analysis, or whatever criterion, to deliberately or tactfully impoverish, and then adjust it unfairly to suit others. Scripture teaches us in something as subtle a scenario as seating arrangements, that where people come to a meeting or fellowship, the poor cannot be discountenanced by being given a peripheral role, or made to 'seat at the feet' of perceived priviledged person, but rather treated not just as another human but with due regard to their significance– in equity. Redefining roles to water down the effect before reassigning it, with a deliberate effect of diminishing importance because of an obvious disregard of a person or group, do not reflect the father heart of God, and this ought not to be. This would be inequality and unrecommendable form of spirituality. This is by no means making a simple analysis of what in often case would be extremely complex situations, with need for gentle and sustained persuasion and understanding to effect desired change. A sense of shared responsibility to see mutual benefits and respect sustained in a group, requires all parties in that group choosing to work together for God-kind of peace birthed in love, beyond comfort zones, each esteeming the other as better– a selfless service. This is no utopia, but a persuasion from scriptures, one that may require stumbling forward, with a honesty to keep learning and growing, as maturing from eating milk as a baby to meat when of age– but not deliberately setting traps with a pre-prepared alibi for a perfect ready excuse, I don't think that cuts it. However in all this, remember everyone is deserving of honour, but there may be those for their office sake would require some level of distinction because God has placed on them a certain level of responsibility that honouring them means honouring God, and this is of a spiritual nature– for instance, as being the 'High Priest' is not everyone's prerogative, or is treating the spiritually mature person as though a babe in Christ without regard to the grace of God on them, or ignoring those in spiritual authority or even secular authority without according the respect due would be also inappropriate [*1 Timothy 2:1-3; Romans 13:3-8; Hebrews 13:17, 9:7; Numbers 12:6-8; Acts 1:21-26, 6:1-7*]. A spiritual leader has to show they recognise this distinction of services as accorded by the grace of God and raise people who similarly accord this recognition, for their office sake, and for preserving non-oppressive structures but promoting loyalty, which is a good virtue. Honouring each other as deserving. Often God's choice may not appeal to us, as He could use weak things or seemingly unmerited, yet we have to honour God in it rather than usurp it, else we find ourselves fighting God with negative consequences on others because of us— I must point out some really do not worry on God's perspective but are bent on building effective structures not fit for a spiritual purpose that put God out of the picture, even shunning God's servants called to them, yet the bible says it is the end that tells, so be encouraged if your trust is in God [*Psalm 73; Luke 10:16, 1 Corinthians 3:10*]. So whatever structure you build must honour God and those He exalts, according to the times and seasons you are in, and love others [what Christ describes as your neighbour] as you would prefer to be treated as well.

lxii.   *Psalm 119:92* shows that the word of God is a reliable resource that keeps your mind fed with the right truth able to guide and preserve. I have heard of stories of people going completely 'nuts' and causing harm to several persons because they lost faith in a system, or community, or school, and were bent on resetting the problem by a very illegal and unrecommended manner such as attacking innocent persons– what I think is needed to any downtrodden is the encouragement of the word of God. It cannot be a proper response to hate out of suffering, or to curse God. To wrongly destroy what you have built because of desperation and attack against you, is not God's way. In difficult times it was God who preserved your thoughts and actions and gave you the right information to live by. How pleasant is the word of God! It has the ability to lift you from affliction, difficulty, trials that would have consumed you. How true this is for anyone, especially a leader who needs to have a right word to give. A spiritual leader can give a healing word because of what they have inside of them, and often the spiritually-led experiences they have received along the way, like the blowing of the wind back and front. To not be consumed by any burden then you must realise that your cares must be in God's hands and draw comfort from Him alone, and let His kindness and loving words minister grace and power to you. One of the blessings of the word is that it fills you with the knowledge of God. Show me a spiritual human filled with the Holy Spirit, I will show you one mighty in the word of God, which would invariably influence their deeds. To focus on God is to focus on His word which brings spiritual growth. The more one focuses on God to know Him, the more of His endless wisdom is divulged and received from Him. [Consider *James 1:25*] It's like one's eyes is being refocused each time to discover what is in a room and to step into incredible magnificence of wisdom. Suddenly there is a painting over there, oh a chair, and over there a stack of books– the sudden illumination has to be tied to sight, the inquiry for information in that room you are in gets deeper, as you peep into what each design means, into what each book hold, and how each meaning intersect with the context of the room and what is without. You think of a great house showcasing the architect and artist. Now consider exploring God's truth, and the journey of discovery. As we see His works we have a clue of Him, though some dare think they know all of Him, but when we meet Him by relationship and spending time we discover more. To hear Him speak His love, His intentions and good graces, then we are moved into more layers of His grace. Suddenly, we realise its been a long way from an outside view, to being in the house, then to knowing the owner of the house. There is the dimension of knowing His acts, but also His ways, as He taught Prophet Moses. And one is not in this alone, there is the family of God. Whereas we have a genuine relationship with God, so also should do with all in this magnificent family of God, made from every nation, called by the grace of God. Whether be creatures or thrones, the wisdom of God is above all and endless, so let's explore together.

lxiii. Genuine leadership is not dismissive of other people's credible achievements, it recognises it, and knows when and what to build on. <u>When foundations have been laid it makes no sense to critic its absence if a solid one. Giving credit when due is a good virtue to have.</u> Be a person who sees good and chooses to give evil no place of prominence. Evil has to be identified and rebuked– but also make sure that good is recognised and celebrated. As much as you can, don't place evil in a prime place, this is because righteousness has to have the pedestal of honour, as a light shining unhindered for many to see the path for direction. To be a leader is to be ready to stick to doing good even when you know history may not deal fairly with you or your deeds acknowledged, often by those who maybe your own peers but rivals– you need not look far. One must value the premise of pure divinity over posterity occasioned by human influence [*Isaiah 5:20; James 4:17; Proverbs 11:1*]. If this becomes the drive, motive can be purer and truer. Frustration sets in when you watch your deeds misrepresented, that is, construed wrongly. A generation that calls evil good and good evil is not true to the essence and core part of God's value system. Any erroneous system that rewards peripheral interests above genuine efforts of labour is unsustainable. God thinks same— it's the one who works that should eat [*2 Thessalonian 3:10, read alongside Romans 15:1, 1 Thessalonians 5:14*]. There is need to be objective about credible success. To think objectively above affiliations-sake is brilliant. It is like applauding to prove a point even if not excited or agreeable, nothing wrong in that per se, as everyone has a freedom to, but is credible purpose not better? If objectivity precedes affiliation we have an even more enduring foundation. Worshipping in a Church is a place to find an example of unity bound by mutual honour of God, as demonstrated in the lifting of the hand and singing is a peculiar way to release and ascribe love to the Lord in humility. God honours those who honour Him. Surely saying to the one who has been kind and generous He is worthy, is credible adulation. Similarly, in our relationship with one and another. To give prominence to a fool to spite the honourable is not demonstration of good discretion or God's kind of justice. Always choosing Christ's way sets the bar higher.

lxiv. Be ready to train for formal leadership but don't neglect your God-given experiences along the way [*1 Samuel 17:36*]. Like David said, when the Bear came I slew it, when the Lion came to devour my Sheep I slew it, therefore in the knowledge of the strength of God at work in me, I can overcome my Goliath! He was in fact saying I have had my trainings from both the lessons of my fathers and tutors but also from my personal experiences. Personally I recall myself, as I write at this time that for about two decades to this present time I have been preaching the word of God publicly and privately, and have had the priviledge of hearing some testimonies of lives being encouraged, healed, demons cast out, supernatural signs and wonders and souls being saved; these I believe I can share because they form formative experiences of enabling the impact that can be brought to many in whatever place, by whatever means. The more we are open to God the more lives can be transformed by His Spirit. Souls are saved when a person believes in Jesus Christ as Lord and their Saviour; yet it is you as a minister of God being used of God as a spiritual leader to spread the message, not you using God. When you get heaven's attention to solve a crisis, or you say something that a person knows deeply you have no access to that information ordinarily, no matter how hazy, but they think you have said enough that points to a credible direction, they worship God realising the prophetic grace– that is God at work, not you in a million years– you having an idea of your mundane abilities. How do you reconcile one's humanness and spirituality? God works in us for His glory, teaching us daily to be like Him. Whether in the 1990s preaching to fellow teenagers, and adults in the streets of Benin city, and moving from house to house sharing the gospel, or in early years of 2000s sharing the word from University Classes to Churches, fellowshipping with fellow believers on our retreats and picnics, or much later in the streets of Birmingham teaching the scriptures, and working alongside the body of Christ here in the UK to reach Christian missional goals, as well as answering questions about faith in other few places I have been– it all adds up to these thoughts bubbling up in whatever places it trickles to. It's the risk we take for being open about our faith, and effort to keep pressing on only by the mercy of God. I recall playing some football with some acquaintances I met whilst on a visit to Guangzhou province in China many years ago, who were friendly to me, and I asked if they had heard of Christ, and they went- 'who is that?' I had to explain a bit more. Immediately I knew there was more work to do in reaching more people globally. Often there is a basis of religion to relate with, and the need for that greater, true and verifiable, that to be known and fully realised. Yet there are many more even in European cities yet to encounter God. Despite the real and present life distractions, looking back to appraise and looking forward, it's a joy to have Christ more evident in life's unique journey- at some grassroots and occasionally prominent places. It is no different when I recently walked into the House of Lords in the UK parliament, for another secular occasion- as I felicitated with others, I felt the prompt in my heart that God could do more here and touch lives. I recall highlighting and sharing with one, the work of Christian Chaplaincy I was involved in just outside of London. I would think often people take leave of me after an event to check on some of my writings and then gain access to the spiritual word- not that there wouldn't be cases where some can't be bothered afterwards. Hopefully at least not after that many questions in the conversation. Yet all these times in the street, corridors, pulpit, classes, offices, industry, recreational tours, homes, schools, on transits, online platforms, advocacy, and so on, it's like running with a cup filled with drink that splatters here and there watering the earth with good seed- it's also like a story that one hears, and when it makes an impression another tends to hear. Somewhat like gossip? Not quite, but good news. And trust me I have spoken to a few hard faces, with louder voices and quick temper that drown noises, whether whilst being handy in practical work or seated across a table pondering on questions, in each moment I believe is a necessary life experience and exposure for the gospel's sake. As a minister of Christ- missionary, I get it, not for the loss of options. It comes with the spiritual territory. Spiritual leaders are aware of that defining moment, that the wind of the Spirit would send them errands and arrange them in strange places for the Kingdom's sake, because your presence and word is needful, and even those that you are connected to will bless lives with you together. As you take responsibility for this pool of grace God brings you into, and as you keep focusing on Him, you will realise you will be more effective by taking responsibility, and not be an easy shrug off. A spiritual leader must master how to abound and 'abase'; and be ready for the next spiritual interruption. Would that be like Evangelist Philip encountering the Ethiopian on the royal chariot on duty, or like Apostle Peter visiting Cornelius the Centurion in unofficial capacity in his home, or encounters of faith in the market square— yet in these ordinary encounters the gospel would travel by the ministry of the Apostles, and bring them to places of notoriety, leaving for us stories of faith and grace. The word of God can be that positively contagious to fill a community, group, nation and beyond. Like in the days of Christ. Yes, several ministers of the gospel are called of God and you may say they all preach wherever sent and have the same role, yet no two are the same, each unique and with different experiences as the Spirit manifests through them, but all operation is for God's honour and glory. We can trust God to be heard within our connections and beyond, and through our resources. However, it is good to be mindful that it is God who brings about the transformation, not us, we all who yield to Him are only instruments in His mighty hands.

lxv. <u>Leadership's essence is the architecture of values, because it shapes people and destiny– an incredible opportunity for life.</u> A framework is a good thing. Who needs a blizzard of 'anything goes?' Coherence, dutiful belief in goodness in hearts dedicated to God can help unlock keys for support of upward moral mobility, of self-improvement through training and affirmation of what is delightful in character. How do we change the culture of a people for the better? Some would say, should it be in another's place to suggest a reformation or turn around as appropriate? What if say such a manner of living or culture is barbaric such as endorsing for instance the death of the innocent(s)? [For example, consider endorsing heathenistic practice of human sacrifice] Then, how do we create a generation that believes in the decency and chance for survival of all people, not a set of gene-types? That would be weird, wouldn't it? How do we see material resource, as a necessity not only for a secluded few but for everyone who chooses to excel? How can we ensure where these positive structures are popping up that it is not deliberately restructured to the negative but protected? How can we ensure the deficient acknowledge it and receive support to engage and excel and not have a smear of brilliance over ignorance, because of futile transient and temporary influence? Somethings has to be more solid than games and divisive rhetoric and vain proclivities. I see it this way— God puts a great premium on human lives, and He understands that for humans to function effectively they have to be run by the right set of value codes, as would a computer system respond to a set of instructions from a relevant software program codes no matter how high-tech the hardware specifications are. Values determine how we respond as humans— you see why training is key? [*Proverbs 23:7*]

lxvi. <u>Practical spiritual leadership knows where the priority is, in hierarchy for obedience and support.</u> [*Acts 5:29; Galatians 1:10, 6:10, Ephesians 6:1*] Please God first then man, not man then God. Remember the scripture talks about seeking first the wisdom of God first. Also, there is the command to be good to all, but first, especially to those of the household of faith bound by the cross of Christ. All are humans, but the believer is bound to another believer of Christ, by a greater depth of commitment made possible by the cross of Christ. God calls us to hate no one and to be good to all. It is the same logic of having a family, then also having a community, but by nature you share a bond to your family, parents, brothers and sisters, first before getting to know others in your community who you should also live in harmony with. You are called to support everyone and speak to their safety but remember there is importantly a responsibility to the immediate group, specific union, or fellowship God has called you to. Helping your brother or sister in Christ need not be to the harm of another who may not be of faith, but it means you care more as to their wellbeing, as developing them is a potential blessing and resource for others– and this pleases God. A spiritual and great leader would be one who understands lasting and transforming results is not from tallying along great ideas or persons, but the spirit of what makes them great or have resounding ideas. It's good to eavesdrop on the great with eagerness to learn, and follow them step by step, even delighting to do what they do and exceed their footsteps, but dear child I show you a much better way– meeting the source. The woman with the issue of blood in the Bible was not made whole because she touched the garment Christ wore, but because she sought the Lord Himself, so virtue flowed out of Him; I tell you many rubbed on Christ in the crowd, but her attitude was one based on faith to be healed, placing a demand beyond the faintest of bodily touch– rather the very hem of His material. An excellent way going forward is seeing that many throng the Lord, determining to lay hold on divine life beyond anything else. The same is true and needs a more circumspect look if the scenario is coming to Christ to gain just intellectual knowledge of His person in history, not entering a relationship, because lives are genuinely transformed when the goal is to seek Christ Himself not only being part of the frenzy around Him. Seeking Him and the blessing that comes from Him, rather than being sceptical. In that moment He fulfils their quest and satisfies the taste for the supernatural and real knowledge beyond academic head-knowledge, because where head-knowledge without Christ or with a similitude of spirituality it is periphery at best, as it bothers on the seen or what is always logically comprehensible, not the unseen or miraculous, hence not good enough.

lxvii. <u>Sometimes it is important for a leader to create 'objective success–' such that meets the stats, one difficult to disprove.</u> However, that kind of tangible success should not be your motivation but rather credible legacy that touch lives positively, it is only needed on some occasion to stop mouths, and to establish some undeniable proofs. And that comes in different forms. It's like a football team that plays so brilliantly but always fail to win, they hold a 90% possession, hit the bar thirty times, win tackles professionally with no fouls, but ends up losing by a goal. If this happens somewhat similarly for a number of double digit games, soon there will be outcry for changes– tactics, manager, pitch, even food plan. Some will say something has to give. That will take someone experienced to create a pinpoint leap. Having the best players or the most entertaining game will soon weary the spectators and supporters if no good results. Same for the Striker in a football, sometimes contributing to the team is great but hitting the goals is preferred, at least as a dominant philosophy– for example having ten seasons run with no goals or assist for a Striker also raises issues, some would think. Logically you say they are brilliant if they give 100%, and may tick all the boxes for the manager, but also they may need confidence from their play, and to shut the mouth of their critics. This is why I say 'sometimes' because quality always exceed results, but it also has to be quality that produces results. Quality should produce good results if not interfered with, despite popular opinion, it may take time, be delayed, but it will speak good things in the long run.

lxviii. On 7/02/17 (the seventh day of February two thousand and seventeen), whilst at this stage of my writing of my manuscript, I felt something in my heart, which is true– 'I believe God prospers. I expect to see it. I stop whining my mouth. I am anointed for prosperity– all round.' Amen. I do think it is essential to also teach the relevance of prosperity to the believer of Christ, as *stewards* of this blessing from God. Establishing its from God and understanding the purpose is for glorifying Him, through supporting the building of His Kingdom here on earth. Unravelling that it means financing the Church, supporting the poor or weak, building healthy families and providing for them, leaving an inheritance for our children, supporting community development, tackling systems opposed to sustainable development and best practices for the good of all. As finance is relevant for all of this, it is needful to embrace God's purpose for financial leadership. <u>Consider being sufficient and being able to be a blessing and raise the aspirations of others</u>. That would have to do with being able to be outward looking, not always inward looking or self-absorbed in a self-preservation mode, that you forget to care for others or the details in your environs— aesthetics, animals, futuristic projects, delightful hobbies. I think more often this would require more discipline and personal interests than having more than enough to spare, but sufficiency could help the switch from survival mode to thriving. Wealth is not for materialistic obsession, prideful living, oppression of others, or for purchasing spiritual gifts or love— as that will be a counterfeit and false gift. Wealth is to be created not stolen from others through deceit, leaving them impoverished. And it is meant to be used rightfully. We would need the wisdom of God to be creative and invest. Godly wealth is meant to endure and bring solace, but that of the wicked man or woman will feed the wind and be vain completely. A spiritual leader has to be able to discern and teach others that wealth is good for you and others generationally and relationally, but it is the abuse of it that one has to be wary of– be careful of any who have self-esteem issues and only feel confident when another is impoverished and unable to be of help.

lxix. When leadership is grossly compromised it is good for nothing but to be replaced; but the one replacing or orchestrating same must not be compromising in due standards too. How can one appointed to a function serve another function, contrary to core and rooted interests? Can a military General of an army be one of another nation? <u>Spiritual leadership bears the interests to the one who gave it its mandate</u>– you think it is solely in the people, and yes you say well, but it is God that inspires hearts and determine the outcome of lives in His sovereignty. First your honour is to God. For without His life, you have no leadership nor mandate. First things first. When God has given the leader a mandate, it is then reflected in the choices of decent God-fearing men. There could be democratic human mandates that have no God-bearing, if majority appeals are always the standard. How about when an unethical practice is popular? This may not be always, especially when often there is a public outcry for good reason. How about a construct that considers spiritual principles that honour God, even when not comfortable. God wins always in the long run, whether good or evil choices are made by some, but God's win is not always your win. Your true win is when you obey His desired win. That is why you can then say, 'God's win, my win.' If God chooses to opt out of a plan, don't desire to win in it. It may appear He has taken a losing side, but I assure you, you don't want a win God has let fail. I think God always wins because He rises above men and is not dependent on time, space, or all known influences. You struggle to win but never asking if your win may mean your loss? Loss of influence, loss of time, loss of friendships, loss of life and family. Far from simplistic– even where gains are made tangibly in these cases without a God-approval. Growing means the willingness to never boast in self but to learn and make adjustments to honour God by winning in His terms. How about that? Salt has to retain its value.

lxx. Permanently protesting you've been ostracised may point to you not haven taken cognisance of the worth of your singularity and of the willingness to give space to those who will validate and gravitate towards you– I think at some point someone somewhere will have to pause and celebrate where they are at and not forever negotiate core values to win persons who thrive on your absence and prefer it so. <u>Taking leadership of you, is giving chances to belong to what is essential, but not making an idol of relationships or groupings, trusting that after several attempts to give love and its rebuffed, that you will pause and be thankful for your essence and redirect it elsewhere;</u> where this is a case of a totality of denial or rejection, as opposed to one who their self needs some form of emotional support and struggling with external pressures and needs reassurance too, then patience is a virtue. A person may have aspects of their character worth commending, and some grace needs to be shown, but there is another kind of person who may not be open to loving and demonstrate zero tolerance– pray for wisdom to tell the difference between these. When the real you emerges through the fire, if of substance it will shine brightly and be purified. Rather than forced licking of boots, how about choosing to create your zone, and joining willing teams, creating a faith chain of possibilities– and then see yourself do great things. Why be a slave with a known foe, than share cheers with a stranger willing to be a friend? I think oppression should be resisted by all good and God's people, without giving it the priviledge of normalcy. This should never be about wealth, but about principles based on value put on people. Christ meets us not on the basis of how poor we are, or rich, but on the warmth of His heart. But if we harden our hearts and reject Him, we stay His hand not because He prefers. For God to foist Himself is not love, but the rape of a soul– so He offers us a choice to choose life and live. Do you still not understand? So, when is the limit of ceasing to try? Similarly, move to love all people. Breakdown biases of hate based on rumours, tribe, colour and your little box notions of self interest– see clearly and keep your options to improve, and be open to being gracious to all in love, within the boundaries of good conscience, reason, and God's laws. Then observe the responses. This will give you some direction, from their fruit, you will tell what is good by the Spirit's help. Hold to that which is receptive and nourish it. In basics, if you extend a greeting and where it is acceptable norm to express some warmth but it is not accepted, persevere and continue, but where it becomes that your recipient is overtaken in pride as one solely deserving, and you being made a fool or 'non-entity,' as irrelevant, to be trampled on– then reconsider your responses. [*Luke 9:6; Galatians 6:1; Matthew 18:16-17; I Corinthians 5:11-13, 6:1-2; Matthew 18:22*] One point, because it does no good to be overly exalted, secondly, it makes mockery of your value as having low self-esteem and overly seeking attention and affirmation, it robs the world of a godly example, it is bereft of good sense known to men, it violates spiritual laws of authority and humility– so please reconsider, and hold your peace, pull yourself together and greet someone else. You're no victim to repeatedly cry foul, it empowers your agitator to insist on an unhelpful attitude. If you give a moral lesson, great– but don't force obedience to unreasonable ideals. Control in this circumstance means, you can do you, not another; real control means you can place a demand on you not another. Loss of control is when you let another's acts actively and unthoughtfully determine your response, inconsistent with your character. What you respond to should be a product of your ideals, decisions, evaluation, your purview and even timing. If you don't do this you will be like the wind, blowing in directions against its will, constantly flaring up, emotionally imbalanced and soon to be wrecked. I think there is a better way to do life. Not necessarily being emotionally constrained, but in a healthy way emotionally managed, and grace filled, undertaking tasks because you have subscribed to it and decided to. Even where in a very difficult situation were working with a very unhelpful manager or team or employees, whatever the situation, know there is a contract stipulating safeguards, it may tilt on occasions– but remember usually it is temporary and you may be able to renegotiate terms or leave for a lesser option with your dignity and health intact. And were you choose to ignore insults, it is because of the strength and wisdom within you, and great ability of control, this is a gift that comes with perseverance and could see you achieve goals others hitherto hadn't, with posterity justifying you. So there is never not a way if God says there is. If is a person is recalcitrant to be of help or to include you in their inner group, then moving on is an option, to pull up or launch new terrains. Many have crushed their souls by accommodating this nonsense of seeking at all cost to gain fatal approvals from those who clearly do not want to walk alongside, in the name of inexcusable loyalty, that will be a fool's errand. The only thing you owe is to love, but not beyond what God's standard is. If you over step God's boundary it would be to your ruin, your proteges' and society– which is unacceptable. It does not mean giving no chance, it just means seeing when a person or group are staunchly unrepentant. Drawing from the Lord's counsel, if another sins against you, we are to forgive endlessly, but Christ's admonishing encourages also efforts be made to reconcile and speak with them, if such will not listen and be reconciled, ask someone else to join your plea (I presuppose this will be God-fearing people because they have to have a healthy value system, not a group that will for instance advocate slavery or trafficking)– then Christ say if this person still will not receive your counsel or that of others, let such be cut off, like someone never known before– now that's heavy stuff. I think Christ was teaching us today to be mindful of those who yearn so much for affirmation, that they forget God's comfort, and also giving forgiveness shouldn't become a mockery event or game that becomes meaningless, if its always going to be trampled on– a time comes to withhold and say, not any more. Christ knew people need to realise the need to seek forgiveness but also understanding reciprocity and willingness of hearts, not think Christians have no choice. God leaves us an example– in death, an unrepentant unbeliever will have no remedy in the grave, as the time to believe after numerous appeal from the spirit, the opportunity was in their lifetime. [*Hebrew 9:27; Ecclesiastics 9:10; Revelation 20:12*] Again, Christ warns, not to throw what is valuable to that which would not value it and tread on it– because it will not only tread it but rend you as well. This is the character of a vile person– the pride in wickedness. It doesn't matter if it is to 'dogs' or 'pigs,' it is the same thing metaphorically, except you want it to be a play thing. So the higher wisdom is, a gift has to be fitting for the intended recipient. What is holy, precious, a pearl, of great value, has to be given carefully to who will appreciate it, I think that's the essence. [*Matthew 7:6*] Apostle Paul in the same spirit of wisdom, encourages us to take note of those who cause division, and avoid them. God's patience with us is not eternal but He is longsuffering. It is disheartening to see innocent people suffer, and constantly ravished and cheated, and insulted. They become so vulnerable and crack, before destroying themselves. Good reason is to be wise and let God lead you. I have heard of cult-like groups in some unspiritual churches that kind of suggest people depending on their looks or age range, cannot join a bible fellowship (obviously not a receptive soil), and subtly and obviously make it possible they don't stay. But seriously, God's house as a place of selective welcome and merchandise? Shouldn't what the place represents speak more than what a few impose— especially if contrary to the heart of God? Well, if true, there is need for an overhaul. This would be a terrible suggestive pattern for a city or nations, to make it impossible for certain persons to thrive, whether they be in minority or majority in that community, that would be sinful and lead to unproductiveness. I counsel and advocate such would be unhelpful, sinful and retrogressive— so I speak against it. Social justice and healthy spiritual growth would also mean creating an environment for human interconnectivity and equitable economic opportunity where people can harness the abilities available in their community. Also ensuring access to priviledges through being able to access the infrastructure or basically groups or institutions. Seek to love and make the move to, if not accepted, identify with those who do receive you. See the responsibility 'to accept,' and on the other hand 'to join,' as on a spectrum, but at some place could meet at the middle to create harmony in the long term. You don't have to give space or forsake your godly heritage, let those uncomfortable leave, dig your foundations where you think you should be and let the haters find their space, simple. There may be a time God may require you let go, because He is bringing you into a large place, then choose not to fight over a well, but like Isaac dig fresh wells– trust God to know when to march around walls to claim territory and when to retreat and move into installing a new assignment. You cannot be controlled by those who will not allow good reason. Heal your Church, heal your community, heal your family, heal yourself by the grace of God. I have found that often hate or being snobby is not a matter for a particular demographic– say, all 20year olds, all white, all black, all brown, all yellow, all female, all male, all poor, all rich, all unemployed, and so on– whatever terminology people assign; as rarely is life experiences squashed into such essentialist or minimalist type argument, that its of one even predominant attribute– you may have to decipher that though a person may be in one category they may share a different or similar quality without contravening that core uniqueness; being strong and muscular may set you up for some sporting activity [either as a man or a woman], it may not automatically remove you from tenderness of heart– strength can coexist with control. God has birth you with an incredible gift to be thankful for. From the beginning of Scriptures, we see the plan of God to create man in community meant to grow, in creation, in the spiritual cosmos, in ability for creative flourish and tending potential. I think also more thought has to be given presently to more encompassing broadness of thinking of acceptance within godly confines, and definition that allows for more mutual harmony between people and cultures as far preferable, for inclusiveness. This helps to form your categorisations on something more authentic, from beyond that only visible. The understanding that says there can be something good beyond our often restrictive paradigms– 'something good can come from Nazareth.' Leadership then as inspired by the Spirit is looking deeper to the core of the person inside, than the outer or facial 'descriptives'. I then connect because I can identify with a grace filled attitude. Well, there are those who connect on the basis of the extremes of what they suppose Christian belief suppose as negative, looking out only for what they think should affirm their world view, not looking holistically and to the clear meaning of scripture. The bible teaches that light will find no solace in darkness, one will melt away for the other, actually dispose of it, put more strongly. Light dispels darkness, causing it to flee. The sexual pervert will find the one morally upright has no connection to such practices, so will the fraudulent financial expert with the poor or notable person not find affirmation. At some true level you will see the disparity, so at least connections can be drawn for the person exploring life and willing to change and accept others. Self-leadership in this instance is finding your place, knowing your worth, that it is alright to tolerate opinions different to yours. And walk alone, if need be than give up a holy conduct, and to work with those who value systems that are healthy. I must say, that rarely would you find yourself isolated, there will be people of goodwill who share your views as well and would encourage you, not everyone will have a disparaging comment– remember, in multitude of counsellors there is safety

[Proverbs 11:14]. And make no mistake of thinking that always the lofty and glamorous are always vile, some may be childishness and inexperience. It may shock you to find that even amongst the poor you may find some horrible level of wickedness and evil that stops mouths. Even among your kin you may get unrecoverable and un-rewindable knocks to the chin. Be wise therefore, judge wisely, make healthy choices. Be kind to all and accepting, beyond your skin colour, tribe, regional politics, gender, economic class– you will be glad when your seed brings its' harvest. But don't let the determined wicked person exploit you to self-destruction, nor should you 'self-harm' to make another feel better, work on mutual upliftment. I believe through the grace that is manifold in Christ you can resist evil, and till your last breath be seen walking contrary to it, by faith. God will never forsake or withdraw your identity and place in Him, as you keep trusting Him. Sin will be cleansed by faith produced by Christ's forgiveness through asking and receiving, and which is demonstrated in your determination to do differently. Why die in ignorance when by knowledge you can triumph beyond circumstance?

lxxi. <u>A leader should not labour to disprove godly counsel that he or she has benefited from, to discredit the instrument of wisdom as though they were strangely enslaved of the benevolence</u>. It however will be the hallmark of a humble person who fears God and is grateful to do this. Pride will be to aggregate success to only one's self at the expense of true helpers along the way. To just say they merely advised, but you chose to work it out, is to forget work is not as important as credible and properly directed production of work. As you could labour in the wrong direction and waste sweat for ages if unaided– it's a possibility. I think rightful acknowledgement is good. To say, I could have got the advice or proposal from elsewhere or paid for it is to despise the instrument of sound wisdom or genuineness in support and set a precedent for restraint next time. Surely, there is an iota of deserving thanks to the one who makes godly counsel. Do not say if it was so great, such should have used or applied it themselves but rather brought you in. Most do, but also some of God's servant may face persecution like others might not, for the word sake– their joy usually is for empowering the saints, those made righteous by the grace of God, to do what God has called them to do. Trials may derail some, however this is the point to return the favours or show goodwill. If you refuse, God usually raises help and comfort for His servants from another. Wisdom to the beneficiary– but also wisdom to the giver of tips for upliftment, do not expect reward or thanks from men, help others for the joy of it and then enjoy the blessings God give. You will realise as you give it won't run dry, and God is really all you will need. And if truly with God, you have everything. God will supply every need in unique ways and in good time.

lxxii. <u>Leadership is seeking to understand 'needs' patiently, in order to meet them. To what end is providing answers that are not solutions?</u> This is why the work of a spiritually driven person is vital. It does not necessarily satisfy what may seem the obvious but the needful. The poor may seem to need riches instantaneously, but God may say let gratitude and self-worth do first, then riches, so their perception of life is not dependent on how much you own or earn. Not that He will not bring in finance or grant your daily bread, but sometimes it is also to learn a good name is to be preferred, and that God's delay is never denial, He is always on time. The values of self-esteem are worthy ideals that some though rich may not have. However, understand wealth is needed and good. Good wealth will empower you and help you bless others and execute your vision. So, to meet a need, think of what should I prioritise? This is an example. To give food to a person in need, some street away, may satisfy his hunger but not necessarily build his/her esteem or sustain their future– that's some temporary respite though. How about thinking more long term, also where such a person is supported through a restorative process back into society. A person needs to be engaged with, greeted in a friendly way, conversed with, treated as a person not a dog, and helped to be all they can be. Adding value to gift. Seeing the person behind the need. A gift, a sincerity, some respect, possibly some directions may be helpful and needed. Some persons may reject a more generous offer for a little with honour. And some may not always be in a good place to give at that present time. But it seems to me, we must train our hearts to empathise– to think, what if that was me? Some may give a little with a great heart than lots to spite. If the ways of the world shift where you dwell, then these values ought to be reclaimed, and ought to be appreciated. That's my take, which I find consistent with the word. Leaving a legacy is teaching the younger generation to place a premium on honourable decisions that are just and worthy. Of course, what is decent cannot be relative to suit self or preferred groups or skewed sense of needful. Even dogs will prefer not to be whipped– so come on, a clear mind will surely see what it takes, that it takes a leader's hand to negotiate through difficult times to bring rightful succour. It is not an obligation to complicate situations. Sometimes the tasty needs a drink. The attention to detail to know if a cold or hot drink, in desert or icy conditions, some blanket or medication, or maybe the need to refer to some professional, takes wisdom. It is not only meeting needs but rightfully meeting needs.

lxxiii. <u>It does not remove from a leader's magnificence to acknowledge his limitation, that someone else has the edge over the matter.</u> Leading a team means the ability to recognise abilities and galvanise both financial capital and human resources at your disposal, and critically sometimes potential that exceed yours, but more because you are able to manage it excellently. Consider not supressing another, because they shine their gift, rather elevate them because they use what they have, for one main reason because where it honours God it is worth being honoured too. However, be wary of the one who displays his or her gifts out of the need to compete or jostle for positions, without the purpose to serve or glorify God. Lifting others up must be necessary even if they are better than you– as true fathers in due time want their children to be better than them, because they are secure in the fact it does not make them less or junior. This I do not think relate to evil or the proud– even God gives uplifting grace only to the humble. Fathers are leaders, in their own class, as other categories are, so promoting their children never reduces them. So is true for mothers. Genuine parents want their kids to do well, exceedingly well, even beyond their legacy– and that positively. It only enhances them– because they can rest a bit more, as competent hands can now do the work. When King David was much older his valiant men took up his fight and went ahead of him, defending him, but remember in his youth he dealt with a Goliath- however, they said to him, we will take care of your battles and shield you- rest now, lest the light of Israel be extinguished from exhaustion of too many wars though God fights with you [2 Samuel 21:7; 23:8-39]. Sometimes God wants us to listen, learn rest and delegation. Christ has raised the spiritual leaders in the body of Christ to be worthy examples of His person, caring for the sheep as a Shephard does, not a 'hireling.' Caring for a people called to reinforce His grace. This is a good thing, raising many leaders unto honour. Never despise the loyalty and affirmation of honourable men. King David in the bible wept over Jonathan in his death, even when as his rival's son, not minding King Saul, because Jonathan was a reputable man and feared God. Scripture reminds us when a man's ways pleases the Lord He is able to bring favour upon a man, which is to be received with thanksgiving. If one can receive a pet with compassion how much more the wisdom of a human? The Spirit's sense is gathering proven people around you, not betraying their trust, or setting them against each other, and to rule where possible. Building trust sometimes take a life time to earn, so don't ruin it by despising honour— it is honourable to acknowledge same. This is a spiritual treatise— requires knowing what it means to be free. Leadership has this intrinsic nature of liberty engrained, of servitude to God and man, one borne of willing conscience. This is not to impose one's set of value system, or to receive forced servitude, but to honour God unreservedly because you've made a choice to, understand the consequences of Him rescinding His mercy as you may become vulnerable to Satan's assault, however from the inspiration and divine support you receive you can direct that to serving and enabling others in need of help, whether practically or emotionally, within reason and your ability. Its loving God and loving people. Loving people as God would.

lxxiv. <u>True wisdom is not succumbing to pressure and affirming evil to stay relevant</u>. Consider the risk of intimidation, neglect of friends, loss of recognition and job, and God forbid the denial of family– but acknowledging Christ in all this must be *primos*, the highest ideal to live for. Accepting and loving your neighbour is not affirming their theology which does not recognise the Lordship and ultimately the divinity of Christ. Hopefully, we can share a cup of tea with them in the cold, sweep the streets together and cut the grass to keep it clean, give shelter as within our means, support programmes for healthy living, encourage healthy families, not denigrate a fellow human being on account of their class, job title, ethnic background, State affiliation, or on basis of whatever ideology they hold– but beyond coming along side people, learning to love them in so many more ways as Christ would have, and has loved the world. As a people worthy of condemnation, he however did not celebrate or affirm our sin but us. God loved the world, humanity, though in the same breath rebuked sin. Teaches us a great lesson for life. Incredible, isn't it? He commands us to love our neighbours we see everyday and God we do not see. In our community and beyond, to be a Christ-witness, making a positive recommendation. A light in a dark place– important to constantly reiterate that in working with others, specifically those that are not of faith, it is not affirming as true their perspective or adopted theology, or endorsing their presumed spiritual activities, or partnering in idolatry prayer with them in agreement, or defiling sacred or consecrated practices to praise-sing a person(s). It seems to me on this matter, great care is required. It is sufficient to be tolerant of others' views, of their right to make such, but not receiving it as scripturally accurate. You would also hope others recognise your priviledges on this regard too.

Christ reminds us that His house is a place of prayer, dedicated to His name, and not for materialism or idolatry, or any other form of honour that do not Glorify God or acknowledge His principles. Our worship must be sincere and flow from the heart. If someone choses to act differently, contravening a set pattern, we can in love seek to restore but not force against one's will. The Samaritan's story shows us that loving another willingly is vital in relationships, being one without religious compulsion but fundamental love for a fellow human caught up in distress. If someone needs a job and you are able to offer, if you consider the human need and help without the condition to them of being spiritually saved first before they can access such help, you do well, because the choice to receive Christ shouldn't be of one cajoled or manipulated into by gifts, it has to come from a place of understanding the depravity [sinful state] of the human condition, of the need for God, of the overwhelming love of God available to all who believe, of the sovereignty of God and His instruction for obedience, of a soul thirsty seeking to know the divine in the highest form, of the maker of all things existing beyond limited self, of the grace of God that has beckoned to us and is mightily at work through His Spirit even today to transform and empower with spiritual abilities. Even though the spiritual benefit of Christ will mean more, they must choose what is more needful– either that which will perish, or that which is eternal. We can hope that through kindness many can see the Spirit of Christ's love at work, and like a holy fire be drawn to the sight to hear God speak from it, like Prophet Moses experienced in Mt. Sinai. Kindness is not a tool to manipulate belief but can be an instrument to draw others to a loving God who can change lives and teach wholesome, un-conflicting, uncompromising and durable truths.

lxxv. A leader prioritises credible ideas over products. This is because ideas drive innovation. And should product get destroyed, the blueprint can recreate substance. Whilst product may be brilliant, there is the risk of it being static except further idea causes it to evolve, though it remains a proof of a workable idea. A real current workable idea could in seconds displace a once booming product. By idea I mean one which is demonstrable, workable, not just opinions, but proven and conclusive decision. What makes the word of God great is because it is an idea that can rule the world and has been proven for centuries through its testimony, that it can produce results. The word of God may seem abstract to the undiscerning, but it is potent enough to decipher situations and bring healing where applied rightly [*Hebrews 4:12*]. This is the greatest form of idea– of that which is ultimate and supernatural in the form of a divine being that brings deliverance to human souls and hope of eternal life. What a revolutionary idea– even more powerful because it is true and fruit-filled. <u>A spiritual kind of leader has to hold the bible as a credible idea</u>. Even beyond, as that which is proven and practical. Don't only look for exceptional events or suggested miracles, rather check on what basis, which idea does it rest on– that way you can tell if it is counterfeit or not. A God-idea will produce a God-kind of miracle and healing. Christ forms the fulcrum of true Christian worship and philosophy.

lxxvi. A good leader that adheres to spiritual thinking should resolve in the heart on how to repay a moral debt. Not that usually because there is compulsion to do so from anyone who has gratuitously extended kindness towards you, but that gratitude would always be a lovely gesture in return, than conspiring to shut down any trace of such love, as perhaps it shows that you were at the 'mercy' of one once, that your pride forbid that it is shown you were once a beneficiary rather than a philanthropist exalted in a donor position. What a thinking? This is not the way to do life, sometimes you receive to lift the spirit of another, not necessarily to meet need always, but in fulfilment of your responsibility to love. Why connive to repay good with evil? To what purpose does that serve? Though, being fixated on fixing permanently yourself as not 'owing' anyone any love or wanting to receive, is troubling, it is perhaps also worrying if you are portrayed as permanently deficient growing up to be needy– the spiritual responsibility is how to honestly create a future of possibilities, of thanksgiving as appropriate, using the wide range of creative outcomes available to enhance lives. If one will boast in their ill-conceived gift, couldn't you reject it or send in commensurate terms– the return, the present worth of the gift with a private note? There is for sure a way to tame the waywardness of what has become a bait. But where it is shown that what has been done was done in good conscience, surely the reciprocal response will be to celebrate what is left of goodness in the world, were it is so rare, and then give thanks as due. The scripture warns it is wrong to call good evil and evil good. It is wickedness to set out to break spirits by refusing to acknowledge any gesture of love shown, especially when in good spirits. It is not for you to decide all the time it will make the other too proud— what if you get your assessment wrong as not always 100% accurate, or this rule not evenly applied, and thanks is withdrawn. <u>You're to be the arbiter of grace for all that is lovely. A thank you is fair to the one who steps out to be nice, lovely and warm towards a fellow soul.</u> If that is a worry to you, how about the impact of returning a gentle morning greeting, how about a wave and not much words, a smile and perhaps not laughter— smaller but better than none, even though I feel the reciprocity of love has done no harm when true and timely. I must say the dread of failing to be grateful when people go beyond their bounds to show grace is that it hardens their hearts and they almost rightly may not attempt to do so next time. Shouldn't one be consistent and just be decisively kind no matter the weather, but also not grant pearls to those who don't appreciate and be stuck in an awkward situation? What then should be done? It seems reciprocating an obvious extension of kindness is a good start point. But not limited, as there must be a preparedness to go beyond what an unbeliever would do, loving those who love them– ours is a higher calling, we need God to instruct us on the limits, so we don't mock grace and make a difficulty of that scenario. My counsel, is to consider God in our attitude so those whose hearts are open do not become weary of doing good. Also think, how about not expecting reward, but basking in the satisfaction of honouring God. There are those who sever ties after receiving generosity not because of the pride that comes of not wanting to be a recipient but the possible shame if another retells the story, so they feel as if grouse-stricken that it is not worth mentioning them as a reference point, because their memory leaves no good trail worth celebrating. That's being too hard on one's self. This attitude must not derail a commitment to good works. An example is, if a child receives a very expensive gold coin from the father, you would expect a thank you. Or lets' say some other form of inheritance. If such a child on becoming an adult, begins to ridicule the gift and insist it could have been more and failing to retain the attitude of giving thanks, that behaviour will cause shame. Don't you think so too? Truth be told, such memory of goodness once shown may be erased from the books or videos, but the fact it was given at the point of need, in that now forgone time, is what makes the 'retain-ship' of thanks appropriate. To say someone else could have done it, or raised me, or given to me, is not good— especially as they cared for you. Consider [*Isaiah 45:10, Ecclesiastics 6:3, Ephesians 6:1-2*]. Often, we thank God, and forget to thank those used of God as instruments, those we see. It was in obedience to the prompting of the Spirit they obeyed, and for being allowed to be used of God— thanks. Not every Parent[s] cares, so for those who do, no matter how little we think their care is, thanks is appropriate, and even for those without the means or maybe given to any disability, you recognise that which is a blessing with them. Reflect on your associated experiences, life's journey, and the posterity you seek to create, and work at a continued relationship as possible in peace. Seek to return the favour of their care, not as a rule or forced necessity, but of love and deliberate compassion, according to your ability. There is evil in the world, but never mind, what is important is if you want to be a spiritual leader taking leadership of your affairs with a different edge, then, teach yourself and others to appreciate what was done positively to them. Be focused and intentional on remembering. If any will not accept thanksgiving, at least you gave it. But don't die as an old and grumpy unappreciative fool. Be wise dear friend. God hates that, most good manner people do as well. When families appreciate each other, or even secular companies celebrate staff, they do that out of sound principle. Think of a nation that not only reel out obligations to her citizens but have mechanisms in place to say thank you to the elderly for service, and also support the veteran of war— that is a nation that will have its' roots established. Do not severe relationships when you have sucked out the juice, giving back is saying thank you. It is more about the heart than the size of the gift. Understood? I'm sure a big heart and good size would be welcomed. And that with a thank you, both ways. To have a difficult day when you don't feel like returning a good gesture could be understood, but it mustn't degenerate into a habit of ingratitude, I think with discipline that takes cognisance of the need of reciprocity, one's character can be fine-tuned to be appreciative, even of things you could have arranged into the proper place yourself.

lxxvii.   Find likeminded people that will strengthen your heart, your convictions that are ideal and sound. I call this the interactions of faith. Have this time to speak positivity into each other. What are your goals? Have you thought through it? How do you plan to achieve it? Then don't stop there– go for it, fight for it, trust God to help you. Let it not be only about you, but the blessing it will bring to you, your family, community, nation. Alright. It may be hard to find that synergy every time, but there is a key, what is positive and good may mostly also tick the box across these categories, such that you are blessed by it, but also those around you. So long your lofty dream is not about immorally or illegally displacing anybody, but such that you have the time, energy and preparedness to work towards your goal. Choose to speak with others who share similar goals that have a non-jealous spirit, and are making progress on their goal aims, they could help your way. That you may be impeded, do not diminish your creativity or calibre. Sometimes even just the attempt towards moving in the direction of your goals could be pleasing, but the real deal is achieving the main objective. You can build confidence by believing that you can do it. It is ironical that some who may say have confidence, behind, laugh at the prospect of your journey, but they have a right to, so rather focus on making a progress to that dream and jumping that hoop, as people could be fluid in feeling, they may change their mind with the glimpse of positive breakthrough. I suggest ignoring the double drama, and get your work going forward. Believe in a God who does the supernatural. He shows seeming puffed-up persons of influence the limits of that they trust, the futility, whether small or big– this reshapes our thinking to realise there is more in the fraction that is within our control or grasp. Who knows, your drive and willingness to your goal may even spur a generation of more than thousands, hundreds of that and millions of millions, to exceed your goals and reach theirs. That is a good thing. Now you not only achieve your goal but aided more to theirs. The scripture teaches the vision may tarry but it will speak and not lie. If only we had spiritual eyes, we will see that often God works in incredible ways to get the maximum glory, and He empowers the strength to walk the walk and talk the talk.

Some may even choose more difficult terrains, especially when part of their destiny, and also unshakably hold sound values and principles, in this there must be the care to not heap praise on one's self but to see that it is God that has empowered this same ability. So, the frail is not reprimanded for not doing more without considering one's own self. Also, one must not oppose the truth, in essence, have healthy expectations which is built on faith, and work with those who pull you up, not bring you down.

lxxviii.   Be determined to be happy for genuine joys borne of righteousness than to commend evil doers, working for wickedness, or in pretence. Choose to bless God for your victories, even if you think it is small. It is an anathema as a leader to be downcast over doing right, or to throw a pity party over your cause, when some are unapologetically partying over the next hack, the next plot for stolen wealth, over the blatant scheme to impoverish a generation, and that includes poor governance and corruption. What an assault that would be on good conscience. You should, and deserve to rejoice, when your lips speak truth and justice. This flip towards regret in righteousness is not permissible–

why is the righteous afflicted and grieved? Don't allow it to become a norm that those who seek to favour a just cause are ashamed, or insulted for doing good. Leading is taking control of your spirit and saying, I will bless the Lord and His praise will continue in my mouth [*Psalm 32:11*].

lxxix. There is a spirit of manipulation, I perceive, and which I resist forcefully. It is that which seeks to exchange destinies, through false representations, counterfeit alternatives, and mindless fetching for grantable priviledges whilst trading decency and humanity. You have to be aware of this manner of activities [*1 Samuel 15:23, Matthew 2, 1 Kings 3:16-28*]. Where a person lies about someone and to another, to chair a position or casts a spell of hate, such is foolishness. Imagine one gets a new job, and some staff say, 'this kind of person is not needed, and we are scooping on getting such and such out, through active targeted planning, through spreading unfounded rumour and getting others to knowingly participate– so we can get some privacy to do what we do and extra working hours for self with possibility of secured promotion– or whatever potential beneficial add-ons, or for no reason!– or for the simple thrill.' Now that's some bad stuff– wickedness. Because its unity and getting along, but unity in evil, and that's not good or 'cool.' Not all unity is credible [Consider *Luke 23:12*]. It's like an employee cursing a fellow employee for eating 'crumbs' from the table, which such considered a priviledged position, not seeing the error of the whole arrangement, that neglects what is essential in that working situation, and rather should be suggesting that which is equitable, improved, and having compassion on a co-fellow with similar experience of the pursuit for wellbeing, rather than considering such scenario a fitting stepping stool. I think that manner of attitude is wrong– what do you think? See Exodus 2:11-15. You must let God work in you, so you will be refined into all you should be. God will take the best of you, and put it under pressure, then you will witness how much of His strength is in you– but don't be distraught because soon you will learn it is meant to grow you spiritually. <u>You must need to take steps to protect your mind by erecting formidable spiritually inspired mental pictures, and if necessary positive memorial which is a reminder, of how you want to see yourself which is in conformity to God's word, and which affirm every testimony of God's</u>

<u>goodness you have witnessed– this is so you are not sucked into a scheme that ignores your joys and freedoms, and rewrites your history, and highlights only your pain.</u> This is why it is the light of God not any other that must shine in hearts to mend it. This is true for every person who wants to be mindful of God as their father and wants their wellbeing– a life that's not a product of manipulative schemes. And if to achieve this you minimise associations that is founded on this state of affairs and class structures, I think that will be well thought of, except conditions demand you are involved directly or indirectly, then you will need to exercise the wisdom, love, truth and grace of God within that specific context. In life, if you listen, it is not appropriating what is others to your gain, but tending your field, it is enjoying from mutually shared common proceeds willingly within good law. This is a smart and ideal way to do life. Makes sense? We have a call to love genuinely, selflessly– unfeigned. If someone inspires you genuinely they will have your honour. There is no blessing in being a leech or one who mounts surveillance to appropriate another's credits or gainful information, but rather be one who not only utilises the priviledge or genius, but

truly recognises the effort in a way that replenishes. If too difficult to source elsewhere then it is best to dismiss the instructions as unhelpful and common, or make reparations and consolidate on good advice.

lxxx. Leadership is beyond followership, it is authentic investment in another's life, which may take time for them to realise the worth but will surely, as the experience or fruit of that engagement bear testament to your works. Its godly character, its positive influence– this is leadership. Christ was a leader before people came along. <u>People following you and taking interest in what you say, is often in response to demonstrated leadership. The followership was only a visible expression of internal leadership, and some of this is tied to timing</u>. The leader of a few gathered in a fellowship club, or 'invisible many' interconnected via social network platforms, or even if they're unknown persons who have been inspired by you, may meet at a later time or perhaps never do– is still of greater value than being one with misplaced priorities, because the glory belongs to God not any individual or institution. One has to be mindful that they are not compelled to take leadership action only by the necessity of bread, fear, a need for social belonging, unscrutinised chance, curiosity, a self-constructed goal or timelining and pathway without reference to the wellbeing of others. Its great to find a man or woman who others enjoy their company, enjoy the fruit of their lips, and are inspired by their godly character and genuinely feel a connection with, not necessarily because they derive physical sustenance from them, or is such attractiveness dependent on their perceived fame or education. Could we say it is because of the value they place on the life of others? Leadership transcends culture. It is not the sentiment of false loyalty, or saying I submit to the lordship of Christ because the messenger, the other, looks like me, as flimsy as that may be, or because of an unhelpful sense of general wellbeing, but on more concrete terms. I recall when I speak with some persons about God, I want to be sure they buy into the truth not by convincing personality, though I would be happy to refer them to another they may find helpful who perhaps they connect with their looks and vibe, as elementary as that is– winning souls at all cost is the key. I personally would be glad I made an impression, but the real deep conviction must be borne of awe from Christ and His truth. So, if everything is stripped away, Christ still holds you firm. It is a great disservice to what leadership represents to think a great orator who compels others to acts of violence as one who leads. To 'boss' one around by intimidation, or attempt to, will not cut it in spiritual leadership. This may create fears but not engender leadership in real terms. Spiritual leadership is beautiful because you cannot generate an artificial replacement, that suits your pedigree, you will have to consider the person God sent to you and wait for His replacement– this is why some find this kind of leadership sometimes very annoying, because it may be easier for some to construct an image or message that's preferred but often with God it is not so. Because God knows best, if you watch and listen you will realise what was given to you is so much better and meets your need. Prior to Christ's public ministry, performing a miracle in Canaan was not on his list of priorities, in some way He was in the backdrop and reluctant to exercise His authority yet– hidden away, often referred to as the Carpenter's son from Galilee. But on the shoulders of this young man rested leadership, the spiritual leadership for a nation and a people beyond a generation, bringing solace, and solution to a spiritual crisis. Similarly, when the time came for Joseph, son of the patriarch Jacob, who was thrown in the pit by his brethren, and later in the dungeon by the call of a false report, and yet God was with him, so much so that he had enough leadership idea to get him out of that entrapment, and through revelation knowledge interpreted the King's dream and made a contribution to secure the financial destiny of a nation. Do I also write of Apostle Paul and Apostle Peter? Who both from the start didn't look suited for leadership at the hierarchy given their antecedents, but with a change of heart where to reach the Gentiles and Jews. Leadership is heart then throne. And if no throne, the heart stays. The one who wants to be the greatest should have a heart of service. This is why great leaders are still influential, even when they leave the scene or wishes everything that demands their attention go away– they still would get that pull for attention, that desire for their input, and many seeking after them to be blessed by their gift. The force of their gift means they are not insulated from the real world but will usually find themselves engaging and being challenged in practical terms. Rather than being irritated and yearn for your peace and quiet to focus on any task at hand, consider reaching out in love to bless and teach. Often the multitudes would throng Jesus even in His solitude in the mountains, though needing to rest and pray, He knew He had to sacrifice and bless these little ones– who searched for Him, even those who came with cheeky questions to justify themselves. Christ was ready to share love and speak truth to all ready to come, and in some cases rebuke [*John 6:1-5; Luke 18:29*]. The spirit of leadership can be cultivated by the spirit of God. As God wants leaders not only in high places of government, homes, schools, businesses, areas of entertainment, industries- all places and sectors of society. With this kind of forward thinking they will bring honesty, productivity and compassion to decision making, and enhance the way life is lived. I think Christ leaves us a good example.

lxxxi. Its important not to lose the narrative of who you are as a person with a unique finger print and biological identification with impregnably distinct life experiences, or losing in a pointless bid of thinking your soul is another's, and then struggling to take up someone else's identity– as though saying you've done what another intends to do, making it your life's goal. There has not been a you and there will never be. The question would remain what you could have achieved if you dug deep down to appreciate your gift– except you are saying your self-sourced creativity would not have created a sparkle, but what if it would have done, then you stand a painful chance of having lost a whole time of 'would have been creative gain.' Others can inspire, in fact God is the greatest inspiration that you can have, but all this is so you can live out your uniqueness, not another's. <u>You cannot do life thinking your contribution can never be meaningful, that would not be taking personal leadership.</u> Imagine traveling on a road, with no bumps, smooth, and whilst cruising on a leisure sight-seeing journey, you see a diversion, you take it– not sure why, then you come back to the main road, then again you see another route, you take it and then return to the main road, this goes on till the third time. Imagine each turn took 20 years. Imagine, this is a reference to the way you lived life, and God only intended you stayed on the right track avoiding purposeless diversions. Some may not mind being able to enjoy a leisurely travel around a city. But more often than not, a purposeful journey is the call to be made. Even a leisurely journey could be purposeful, and to be distinguished from a completely aimless drive. My emphasis is to imagine a situation, the boast of the driver, is at least I prevented someone else from journeying on that route, or that maybe there is pride of being the few that had journeyed there. I would think that is clueless and belongs to a band of stupid excuses, as it does not match up to the purpose of a route which is for a journey to a destination. There is a joy in being able to say, I ran my race, I reached my goal. It surely has to be better than the thrill of– I got past another car. It has to achieve the objective– a win, a destination, in honour of the rules, or something of significance? For the Christian, life's journey is done in the context of one who will give account to the right judge who sees all things. How has your life improved based on your choices? It would matter more when lived in purpose. Rather than roam around opinions, we know that to do right is a preferred option. There are set laws that speak to our conscience. To not harm the innocent, to be thankful for genuine kindness, to protect the weak and children, to not deal deceitfully, to love those who birth and care for our wellbeing, and so on– making right purposeful choices in our life direction I suggest would be honouring God in these.

God has set this in our hearts, that even before you come to spiritual maturity these basics ring clear in our conscience, whether we heed it or not is another thing. What Christ offers is the strength, will, to obey God which the carnal man cannot do. He changes our heart and purifies a dead conscience. If you want to be a person of godly leadership, be willing to follow God's set path for you, don't turn to the left or right. Except of course He asks you to. If you miss it unintentionally or perhaps with intent in your weakness, then know God wills you back. In fact, He waits with open arms. Often straying from God exposes you to attack. I believe your reading this is a step in His divine plan— how you respond is a choice for you to make.

lxxxii.   As a leader how do you allow persecution not to reshape your perspective from that which is compliant with the principles of the word? For example, not letting bitterness or retrogression set in. Is it the unwillingness of ministry partners to follow through their commitment? Is it in not finding help to engage in furthering the work, or personally you are tired and have rescinded on articulating your ideas? Is it a change in policy in your government that had in some way stifled progress? In all this, tenacious leaders press on, and change strategy, to adjust, but not compromise on scriptural standards. We then don't attack the principles of partnership and isolate yourself from commitments and communities you are meant to reach, disengage from worthy agreements, cripple your church or ongoing revival movements because of all that has befallen you. The preferred option as a leader would be not to give in to unscrupulous demands that circumscribe the rights of others to peaceful assembly and freedom of worship. We are called to disciple men and women, young people, to grow and be leaders, to recognise their leadership potential, that God has put in something in them to be nurtured. <u>One has to then work on building necessary partnerships despite the strain or attack on your spirituality, no matter how low profile the network is, and begin to harness the gift of God in you, rather than work in isolation— except if God calls and brings you out</u>. There are repressive regimes in the past that have given no place to even a valid legal challenge, or impeded lawful assembly, the Church then had to pray and organise lawful resistance to such actions. God always make a way in the midst of such sufferings, the gates of victory is always open the saints of God– those declared righteous by the faith in, and of the Son of God, called to walk in sanctification. We are called to engage in peaceful disobedience against evil, prioritising Christ's values. There is a way, it is the way of the cross– continually trusting God's word.

lxxxiii. <u>Leaders are called to speak the truth in love, not negotiate the truth in love.</u> The ability to be honest, authentic, faithful is rare, and to do so without malice, with a graceful heart that wants to see others flourish is even rarer. It allows those who will otherwise not receive the truth to listen, because they know you have their best interest at heart. The truth in love should be our continual watch– the question is, how can I be loving and not negotiate the truth? I must say, the one who presses you to lie on their behalf will think less of you when another opportunity comes that requires a person of truthful character, and you wouldn't be the choice then as you have shown yourself as swayable. To what essence is talking the truth but without love, if it ruins lives and families? The proud may not accept truth in love but upon reflection, they will surely recognise their error. Truth is always a sword, as it exposes intents. Love makes truth easier to communicate, not less potent. Negotiating or compromising on the truth is proving one's self unworthy of honour. Christ sets an example– when asked who He was, He said, 'I am a King,' He never denied it. To another, when He preferred to say nothing, He kept quiet but held on to the truth of Himself. That you are not vocal to your critics do not mean you have compromised on the truth of yourself– especially if they would not believe anyway if you told them, or might pretend to affirm or believe when such don't, then it would be better to take Christ's clue and shut it in. Christ affirmed His identity, with thorns and suffering, He bore witness to the truth of Himself and His call. This thing called truth, the truth of the gospel, has cost lives to redeem nations. It has also saved lives and condemned lying tongues. Christ was ridiculed as Joseph's son, but it didn't change who He really was– the son of God. Over the years, the truth prevailed. What God says about a person is true and eternal. Holding to the truth then is maintaining God's confession over your life, even if it does not appear so at that present time. Because if God truly said it, it will not fail, and can be relied on. The truth will prevail in the end. For instance, watching a tree grow– say a Cashew tree which bears fruit, even if there is no fruit yet, truth is declaring what tree it is and the expectation to eat of its fruit, until it manifests in the stipulated time. The truth was not when it manifested but it has been true since the inception. The truth of its nature, the truth of its kind. If nothing corrupts the truth, it lasts and fulfils its mandate. Even where it is corrupted to produce something other than intended, the truth remains it was so until affected– it becomes the truth which was corrupted. Whatever the truth was, it is. God's word is true and becomes our truth, as a spiritual leader. God's truth preserves and has capacity to change circumstances.

lxxxiv.   Leadership is knowing when to fight in a lawful and godly way, and when to refrain from doing so. After you have done all in the instructions-book God gave you, then rest. Why press on when He wants you to stay down? Wisdom is not doing yesterday's mandate, but today's mandate, acting on a fresh word from heaven. Lord what will you have me do now? Now. A fresh word from heaven is important in leadership. The word is still as fresh for a thousand years if the cloud of God's presence is on it. When He moves, then move. When He says stay the sword and sing, don't carry on swinging your steel in battle [*2 Chronicles 20:20-22*]. God neither needs the song or steel for victory, it is our faith He needs, our obedience to godly instruction. <u>God help us, if we want to see steady triumphs, then again it must be that it is the leading of the precious Holy Spirit that has spurred us on, nothing else.</u> The question for many is how do I know when to start or begin? This is why I believe a leader must be spiritual, that is sensitive to divine promptings, not always relying on senses. However, God has given us senses for our good to guide us well. We do not need a word from God to have a shower or eat a meal or to exercise, but good sense tells us that this is good, and beneficial. Also, we can show that scripturally good hygiene and physical exercise is of some benefit and a good requirement for good stewardship of our body. The point being made is sense is good, but it must also come under the Lordship of Christ, under the guidance of the Spirit of God. So, if a food brings damage, or a particular exercise destroys my body, so I discern God is not in it. This knowledge shapes my decision. But what of where I need to do something beneficial, but the Holy Spirit expressly intervenes and refrains? Like eating a meal or taking a walk? This is where I reckon, it gets difficult for some Christians, and some maturity will help. Establish first, God can do that. He forbade Apostle Paul from traveling to a particular city to preach the word, for that time [*Acts 16:6*]. In other times, He commanded a fast– abstinence from food for some time in other times encouraged a feast in thanksgiving. It will be naïve and carnal to then insist on 100% good sense and make an argument for nutrition, or in the most important bit of sharing the word, when God has a more credible plan to reach more souls and save lives. God's agenda is always greater, so we are to listen to Him to become more productive. That's the goal. Again, our sense must be managed in such a way that it does not negate the freedom the Spirit brings. The Spirit of God do not intend to make slaves of us, but to make us worthy ministers of service to all people. Christ in obedience to Father God knew when His time had come, when to proceed to Jerusalem, and when to stay away from the city, in those days. Same way in God's dealing with Joseph in Egypt in the time of Christ's birth, same with Abraham in his journey. Also, I must add, what if your restraint from the spirit sounds elementary, as in the daily things– but consider, what if your food has been poisoned but not to your knowledge, and the Holy Spirit says arise, don't eat that tasty looking cake, from that generous hand? God has saved some lives this way, I know.

lxxxv.   Allegiance and alignment is something to think about when in the place of influence. To consider, who do I owe my allegiance to and how do I come in alignment with a godly purpose? I do think its not enough to insist on cultural or institutional allegiance at the expense of godly alignment. Some may say for instance, the Church has taken some artistic and social feel, but it is for true believers to debunk that where it is a heavy criticism– because it is such that focuses on a stereotype rather than considering the aspect of experiencing the beauty of our uniquely varied gift or diversity of gifts. We cannot make out that if another person is not like you they are not fit to be saved, or utilised for leadership, that would be an anomaly, most would agree. We cannot reduce the election of God to skin colour, that would be painfully empty and misleadingly constructed theology– as coming in alignment to the wholesome purpose of God means forming allegiance with heaven's rhetoric and action. Both the opportunity for a leader to serve, and the priviledge of receiving service must be open to all of God's people, not just because they belong to a man-made club that sets its criteria to deliberately be obnoxious, or on strict terms as colour, fund, age, gender, or even diet preference– without an iota of preparedness to be open to the possibility of God speaking and making an exception to whatever rule is set. Of course the element of reasonableness is required in these things, as an infant can clearly not speak, or an adult may need to learn a new language when moving to a remote culture; but consider the notion that it has to be the youth speaking to the youth, or the elderly to the elderly– couldn't God work beyond our lines and use the elderly to communicate to the youth, or use the youth in respect and grace to admonish the elderly, without removing from the opportunity to encouraging each other at their level. *[1 Timothy 4:12; Titus 2:3-5]* Sometimes we set arbitrary lines that stifle the Spirit *[1 Thessalonians 5:19]*. It may be helpful to have some guidelines, as smooth as both sides of a single coin with different designs on each side, but not necessarily most expedient- kingdom purpose would utter more. There could be some advantage in teenage pairings or peer group influence, or internal conversations across sections, but not as an absolute. Not even to the extent of turning deaf to the voice of God, that is if there is the ability to hear and recognise His heartbeat. Someone yells, 'God sent me here!-' and the listener goes, 'but that does not meet my preference!' Either one of the two missed the memo, or perhaps for some the organisational rulebook matter more. Wouldn't that be arrogant? Even more, if we think prayer matters less in the things of God. A spiritual leader has to be discerning to say- 'Lord, what would you have me do, so I can get on with it!' I think it is time to get past any inhibition, that which restrains good from thriving, and begin to support causes which are for spiritual advancement in the Christian faith. This includes tearing down walls of racism and tribalism, and teaching others to do the same- and by deliberate and obvious inclusiveness into teams until it jells, until we come to the unity of faith. God took a chance with us, by including us all to His body, with the opportunity to grow into perfection. We cannot demand perfection in the flesh to be included as none would match up, so therefore align to God's will and qualify by the approval of God. Our generation will lose the grip when who is on the pulpit is more important than the words being spoken, or than the visible authentic testament of their faith. We should be able to weigh the words to see if it matches up to Scripture and consider the testimony of their life and witness of the Spirit, to hold them in high esteem. My prayer is that God enable those called to receive, to in humility acknowledge the grace of God when at work mightily. A contrite heart, as the Psalmist say, God will not despise.

lxxxvi. As a spiritual leader in Christ, you must have and understand the spirit of your faith. The spirit of your faith is one based on the finished work of Christ on Calvary. This refers to the substance that makes our faith. The spirit of a thing is the essence, the core, that which makes it thick. Lawyers talk of the spirit of the law, as it goes beyond the letters, to the intention of the draftsman and legislator, also the peculiar origins. The spirit of a matter refers to the foundations upon which it is based. In the same vein, the spirit of faith is based entirely upon Christ. His love for us and how that transforms us. In Romans 8:14, the Scripture tells is that to be led of the Spirit is to be a Son of God. This is of submission, learning under the direction and tutelage of the Spirit. First, we see that to move our faith from just a religious code or religious assent to history, it must be based on one, that is a reliance on Christ, trusting the ministry of the Holy Spirit at work. We receive the knowledge of the word then we obey the truth of it, by receiving those words as true. In John 1, it is those who received Him that are empowered to become sons of God. God's offspring. To possess God's make up and significant structure. This is why some were offended by the ministry of Jesus, because in their affirmation He was just a man and had no right to claim a lineage to God. But scripture tells us that He was God incarnate. In this blessed story we see God's redemptive work through Christ for us. We do not need to argue that we are in a fallen world and that the human race has come under affliction as is so evident, because of sin, but we need to consider more carefully the original intention of God for wholeness, as Adam the first created man was not subject to all this suffering until he fell into sin- why do we then think it is out of place for God to be able to restore a disjointed and flawed relationship? God has regained the believer through the blood of Christ, the Lamb slain for the covering of the spiritual nakedness sin brings.

lxxxvii. <u>Consider this for worthy leadership- being an example to our 'allies' (friends), by our appropriate and temperate response to our enemies and the weak. How we treat those mean to us is a screenshot to those who we are now in good terms with what to expect.</u> It shows them the extent to which we are merciful, so when they too being fallible fail, how much grace we could exhibit, and how willing and quickly we are able to impress strength as capable. Why lose friends over foes? Treat all men so cautiously, and even risk being called naïve, so when at last you disengage or reprimand, even the mean and vile or spiteful, know you persevered, and they wonder what took you so long to react in negation. Let's consider God, who though strong is slow to anger, that some even think He does not exist— though quite spectacularly occasionally He turns up and sets things in perspective miraculously to get a few thinking what possibly happened. And also, to the group God has planted in your life [God forbid they come to that place of human weakness to do wickedly], that your mercy will last longer, and they will be encouraged to bury their hatchets and set foundations with you, and then build your futures and friendships together. God's mercy is eternal, so should ours, but remember there is no repentance towards God in the grave, so it makes spiritual sense to appropriate the grace of God within the time limit for divine access.

lxxxviii. <u>Spiritual organisation is a prerequisite in leadership– to be anointed does not mean to be logistically flawed and strategically defective</u>. God had a redemptive plan from the onset, He didn't wait for man to mess up and start scrambling for what to do. Both His foreseeing and elective grace, and mercy was at work from the beginning, working in perfect synergy. From scriptures we see Christ also took time to organise as purposed by the Spirit. God set out creation at the start and ordered it into days for our learning. Couldn't the sovereign God have orchestrated all things in less than a second, being all powerful? If we believe with God all things are possible, then that doesn't come as a shocker, but we understand often He chooses to organise, compartmentalise, to training us in righteousness to understand work and rest, and in order for us to see the power of a spoken word. So, we see the first, the second, the third day to the seventh– ordered chronologically and whilst resting on the last. It was relevant to have implications in the season of our lives, being intentional about our plans, creatively designing, understanding the place of hard work and rest, demonstrating authority, showcasing the unity of the Godhead, and many more examples. <u>God wants to organise our lives, organise His Church, under divine goals– often this comes as a result of spiritual revival and release of grace. Are you prepare to expand your tent and frontiers for what God is about to do in your life, and reel in the harvest?</u> For Christ– most of His earthly meeting meant preparing Himself, preparing the people to receive and preparing the place. On Himself– being to often withdraw to pray up in the mountains. Sometimes with His inner team of disciples; Peter, James and John [*Mark 9; 14:32-52; John 13:22-25*]. On preparing the people– He encouraged them to follow Him for what was needful, not mere physical bread or just miracles but the word (bread) of life. His disciples were reminded of His death, this way Christ was preparing them to be able to process grieve but also to be thankful for the accomplishment of a heavenly purpose, so they understood the significance of resurrection [*Matthew 16:21*]. Understanding turns grief to joy, complacency to activism, feeble minds to astute scholars, perceived degenerates to productive persons. Once they saw the light, why Christ had to die and resurrect, the awkwardness of why the all-powerful God had to be subjected as a play thing, why their share of the kingdom of Christ after trading off (abandoning) their business and subsequent personal cost of followership was more than an earthly reward but a heavenly one, it all made sense– albeit spiritual sense. Also, Christ made sure He prepared practically, the place He was to be in– consider the prophecies before His birth and the preparation of His last supper with the disciples, His active involvement is evident. Why the fuss over the exactitude of place, room, use of a donkey, timing of entry into Jerusalem, the use of certain items and many more pointers– this is so it would be clear who the messiah is on research in later times, also so we can identify with pinpoint accuracy the fulfilment of prophecy without nostalgia, or see if we are to wait for another. I think His deliberateness in organisation is striking, and leaves most biblical enthusiast thrilled and humbled. The birth of Christ had to be set in a time in history when Israel had no Jewish King in the Polity, for her King was to be in the midst of her. Similarly, the Christ is to live in the midst of us who believe. Our knowledge of Him must transcend what we see in the physical. His preparation for earthly arrival was not to be in the palace or one that secures the pride of humanity in materialism excluding the down trodden, He was to be found amongst the lowly but yet receive generous wealth, including all who come humbly at His feet, also His safety was to be divine, not one guaranteed by kinsmen or the protection of a standing army, also His presence was to bring unity beyond the borders of Jerusalem– 'for out of Egypt God has called a Son' [*Hosea 11:1*]. Even though He sought refuge in Egypt, the purpose of His travel exceeded that. More so, this Christ was to be a gift to the nations, not held back to only the biological children of father Abraham according to the flesh. Christ's gift was first to the Jews, and then to all tribes and tongues (Gentiles) who believe in Jehovah's work. As God's children by faith in Christ being brought in later to the experience of the grace of God do not negate the first's, or make you inferior. Just as an earthly parent would not consider any of their kids as deficient in human life because of the ranking of their birth, or should each of them jostle for acclaim, but rest in their heritage. This is true also in the analogy of the husband and his wife, put side by side in the spiritual context of Christ and His Church (bride of Christ). I think this structure God introduces, is so we can see He orders the end and beginning, to know who authors it and ends it, to see the workings of His grace to all who believe, to learn His discipline so we see how benevolent and yet uncompromising He can be. God often refers to Israel as my first-born, but yet other nations would come into this divine experience much later, and has now experienced the over flowing grace of God. It is as if being led from the outside in. Though the nation at that time herself was under the restriction of the Roman empire in the time of Christ, with Grecian neighbours' heritage and visitors from Ethiopia, and people from other parts, yet God had pre-planned that spiritual insight, knowledge, would arise from this nation bringing liberation, called small yet mighty– and her liberation would be foreshadowing His second coming. The whole scheme is not chaotic. Each fine detail showcases God's great plan. See Acts 17:26-27; Deuteronomy 4:7. Let's be in remembrance too that God has placed all nations and people equal before Him, and is not a respecter of persons. Also, in Adam and Christ case study, we see the narrative of the 'first Adam' and 'Second Adam,' the later as a pillar of redemption, fulfilling the purpose of God set from the foundation of the world. An even more astounding revelation is Christ is the spiritual first-born, the revelation of the father God to whom we who believe are all called into [*Colossians 1:15,18; Hebrews 1:5-6, 2:10-11; Romans 8:16-17; Isaiah 53:10; 1 Corinthians 1:2; 2 Timothy 1:9; 1 Peter 2:9-10*]. God raised Israel as a prototype to show His exceeding resurrection power as He would in Christ [*Zechariah 2:8; Exodus 4:22; John 4:22; Isaiah 61:8-10; Romans 11:11-42*]. I do not make a rule of this principle of organisation and purpose, of God preparing and setting scenes, people, examples, for our learning, and speaking to much deeper things of relationship and the network of His grace, like a finely woven thread into a garment from silk. As we grow we realise things are organised in certain ways for a reason. In whatever way Christ prepares us, either practically or otherwise, it is to ensure we are productive. Christ not only prepares us, He prepared Himself working with the Father, pre-earth and whilst on earth, for His ministry- many where amazed to realise He was pre-incarnate Abraham, and knew exactly He was to fulfil the writings of the Prophets. No wonder the clarity of His work. We all can learn from that. No matter how preposterous it sounds. Often, He was amongst the scholars, teachers, youths, enquirers of His time, engaging with the truth of the word, even though He authored it, knew their premonitions and what would be their response, yet He listened as though He knew nothing and taught them as one with astonishing understanding. He prayed and fasted often, He submitted to baptism by John the Baptist to 'fulfil all righteousness,' honouring God, to demonstrate what His ministry would encompass– His suffering, death, burial and resurrection in the newness of life– in many ways Christ prepares us uniquely for the work He calls us for, whether be through even our own experiences where we begin to see patterns of His hand, but also in placing us with people who will shape us and help us grow daily. Christ through His word and Holy Spirit reshapes us mainly to conform to His person. This is so we are fit for His use. He also prepares us for a prepared place [*John 14:1*]. We cannot occupy our destiny position until we are a vessel which is honourable, walking in obedience, and in His perfect timing. God has things set, before, during and after. I think this sets a good example for you, if you want to walk in spiritual leadership.

lxxxix.   As much as God will grant you grace, stay standing and planted in His will, because 'rootedness' in spiritual leadership is essential; this is beyond staying power in a role, lengthening terms, but walking in par with the Spirit until He takes you from point A to point B. Which may be minutes, it may be years, or decades, but it is about being sensitive to His will. Often as believers you will have to arise again and grow, learn from mistakes and recognise its opportunity to continue growing in perfection. God never wills us to fail or falter, needless say for the purpose of teaching us a lesson. He is perfect and wills us well at all times. God who by grace has made those who trust Christ holy, righteous, sanctified, also calls us to walk in holiness, righteousness, sanctification, they have received by faith in Christ- you've to be planted in to grow in. Your light is called to shine forth and brighter, from the light you have from Christ, in a dark and perverse world, as a spiritual leader. As a tree planted in righteousness, be established, let your roots go deeper, such that every wind will not pull you from your place- as by deceit and vain philosophies of some who have no bearing in God and so do not know His word. There is a sense of your candle stick sticking to where God has placed it. God promises He would not even permit a temptation He knows will break us. It happens then that when overwhelmed with temptation, it is not God that has caused you to falter. But He is there to pull you back up again. I urge you as those committed to leadership to be part of a people determined to stand according to the grace God supplies– this is because in rising and falling is a loss of momentum, fervour, and 'nutrients,' as a tree may although survive, with a slim chance, or maybe not, being constantly uprooted and replanted continually, but it is better if it allows its roots to be dug deep and stay deep into the soil where it is planted in the right place and nourished, and where it continues to grow and gain from its taproot and engaging with all opportunities around it with every stretch of root.

In Christ we have been rightly situated, planted in the vision of His principles, now is the time to not disengage as though dead, or to walk away from God–given ideas and visions– for those areas of opportunity we fail to step into and adhere to will hardly materialise. The truth is, nothing will separate us from God's love for us. However, if we fail to grow in God, or gain root, how then do we expect to profit from His grace? Same, if we pull back from that which God is calling us into, the grace to flourish in that withers, causing unproductivity. If one remains in God, then there is the potential to thrive. Don't nurse the cheeky prospect of waiting to bear fruit and then pulling back, because the key to staying fresh and constantly productive, in several ways, is remaining connected to the vine. There may be times God stops us from engaging in a particular task to redirect us or possibly relocate us, but never will it be to blaspheme His name, or to destroy His divine destiny for our lives. The foundation of God will always stand, we ought to thrive in that. He heals us though when we are found far from home– removed from His grace. That was never His will, but the sovereign God has a miraculous way of bringing us back home, to the place made for us before the foundation of the world. God understands your frailties and often extraneous pressures, so He has prepared a grace beyond measure to equip and root you in His purpose but you must be 'willing and obedient' to bind yourself to that which matters *[Isaiah 1:19]*.

xc.   Take a clue from Christ and do not make functioning within an institution an idol, 'a must do—' make no mistake it could be very helpful to be within an organised structure or system, but don't worship it, and beginning to think that God can't do something spectacular with you or without the structure of men. When Christ said foxes have a home but the son of man had nowhere to lay His head— it should point our hearts to two things. That, one, His ministry was not about enriching Himself and building an abode where He could rest, tied to His name, and could pass on to his immediate family like a political King in the flesh would, it was selfless— what a model for us as believers, there was a greater purpose to His life. Of course, He would have heirs and a kingdom, but the dimension was more spiritual than earthly, there would be vestiges of the effect here, but it would be clear where the authority came from. Also His ministry showed movement, a movement continually towards the goal He was on earth for, a willingness to minister in the synagogue and out of it, in homes, in streets, in fields, to those to whom He was called and were of faith, conveniently, and even to those who derided Him, and made His work difficult and inconvenient. Christ ministered to those outside His circle, like to the Samaritan woman. A great lesson. As a leader begin to think, how you can minister with grace outside of your comfort zone, and out of your inconvenience, as in opportunities may arise within your comfort and without, grace is needed then to heed and to function in both situations. But to create artificial structures that restrict you [even when the Spirit is leading you in a different direction] is actually spiritual weird. <u>What makes you a Christ kind of leader is not your title or numbers of conversion to your name, but your spiritual pedigree, it would take a spiritually sensitive person to discern that and operate in several realms of dimensions.</u> Elijah was much a leader to a nation whilst in a cave and traveling a desert, than a man who was somewhere in 'Ahab-street' selling dates with employees and professing spiritual faith to his/her self-founded fellowship without divine impetus. A Gehazi may later come along to be under his tutorship, but you must understand, if God raises a man to lead He will grant grace for the mission. It is nice when people listen and follow you, but even if they didn't, your spiritual honour remains because you chose to respect God's purpose above the priviledges of man-made palaces, governmental institutions, and places of influence– which is always a joy and fulfilling when they do listen as well. Often in time God raises one, few, or many, to receive the baton. However, it is also the responsibility of the generation of that moment to prepare to receive. This is not to say God does not work within institutions made by man, He does, but He is not limited to it. Even when He creates a system Himself, or give a method of operating at one time, nothing says He cannot change the way of operating and still retain His honour and glory. That He healed the blind with mud today, does not mean He has to always follow that pattern, and not speak to blind eyes to open without laying hands the next time. Moses may have to speak to the rock at one time, and not strike it. One has to be alert to the way of the Spirit per time. We see Christ as a child in the temple learning the law, in His adult life announcing His mission and teaching, even requesting His disciples and some He ministered to, to honour the office of the priest, also He recognised the need for John the Baptist's prophetic role; yet He did not shy away from rebuking some of the leaders of the temple who in those days were called the Pharisees and Sadducees, in strong terms, only because He loved them, and wanted God's praise to be honoured. Even when He entered the temple and drove everyone out with whips He wanted to emphasise what should be the proper code of conduct in worship, not one driven by materialism– how true that statement, that the zeal of the Lord had consumed Him. Many in His days wondered where He got His authority of Leadership from. Often His response was pointing back to Father God. It was spiritual and from heaven. They could not resonate with that kind of talk and reported Him to the secular authorities of His day to be arrested for His activities. Just to say that despite this agitation within the established institution, Christ wasn't being disruptive but rather was sure God wanted Him to speak truth to power and speak for social justice and faith– of the need to take more critical note of matters of righteousness, considering the poor, the fear of God, and opening their eyes to the prophetic times they were in. Behold, the Lord of the institution, Christ Himself, was before them, but they could hardly give Him His due because He had not 'graduated' from their religious schools or grown under their mentorship or tutelage as in those times, agreeing with their philosophies, nor did they have a 'confirming' word of Christ's status. Can't we see it is dangerous not to hear and observe God clearly, and demand others fit in our institutional boxes, whilst choosing to be deaf to the God one claims to work for? This must have been hard for those piloting affairs and desire a smooth running of the temple or 'Church' at that time, you may be forced to think at that time– but how about labouring in tasks and neglecting the warm blessing of the voice and goodness of Christ? Of receiving the blessing of God, but not the God of the blessing? How does that work to advantage in a spiritual edifice? I think we must look around our immediate circumstance and be deliberate about not impeding Christ in the way He wants to work amongst us. Does it begin by asking God's spirit what He wants to do first of all, and being sure it is God that has spoken, confirming it amongst the brethren? Doing away with some tradition and trust a new move of God? Working beyond set lines of culture, and taking a step of sacrifice that honours God? Maintaining ancient marks and testimonies of God's grace and not rewriting it to sooth our ego, or renegotiating the grace of God? God is teaching us the need to not get so busy with operations and forget the God of the work. When Christ had to speak truth to the powers that be, in reality He was speaking the truth from the place of power, as He is Lord of the work, and so was instructing not appealing. Shouldn't this call from trembling and inspire a rethink? You see if we knew God was Lord of the work we would adjust our tendencies, blueprint, or maps, even if it was a sibling or stranger that instructed us only because being a messenger from God– for God's sake. However, it takes maturity to discern when God is at work and listen; that way we find ourselves working and walking with God when we obey, not thinking and acting against Him. That said, it is better being in a structure God is in, than walking in isolation if God is not in it. The core emphasis is, whether God orients it.

xci. To be under the leadership of the spirit is a sign of submission to God but also spiritual maturity, showing you have been moved from being a child of God to a son of His– growth. John 1:12 speaks of salvation, those who receive Christ have the authority and right to be called offspring (children) of God, as they are born again spiritually, because this is not a product of fleshy and love exercise, but a spiritually graced service *[Galatians 3:26-29; Romans 8:14]*. Christ grants us the priviledge for sonship and relationship with God. Let us understand that to be a spiritual leader you must be born of God, and belong to His spiritual lineage, and then grow into maturity to lead and fully exercise your authority. Union with Christ is essential and coming into maturity is key for leadership, evidenced in believers allowing themselves to be used of God, not being a babe but one in service. When we are saved we don't become adults in the spirit immediately. As there is a birth process which comes by faith so there is a growing process. I receive this by revelation, and I also find it consistent with the word of God. I have also heard some honourable teachers of the word also teach on need of spiritual maturity. Before one is saved the Holy Spirit already begins to brood over one's heart drawing them to the Father, as would a barren and dead earth, and where they do not harden their heart as the revelation of Christ is made known through the voice of the Spirit, He comes in and changes their heart– from one which is stony to one made alive. He nourishes it as water does a dry land, and as fire consumes impurities. God gives spiritually newness of heart as you trust Christ. You can then come into maturity in the things of the Spirit by continuing to feed on the word of God, growing and widening your boughs, moving from having milk to dining on strong meat– as Apostle Paul describes it. From being carnal in understanding and perception to being spiritual, so you can enjoy the fellowship of Christ more fully. You can't step into the fullness of the blessings of God until you've attained maturity, and this requires walking in submission to the spirit of Christ and in consonance with His timing. Consider Galatians 4:19– 'my little children, for whom I labour in birth again until Christ is formed in you.' So you want to think differently, and not be held down? Switch from childish thinking to manly thinking, hold your thoughts down, pin it to how Christ thinks, stop it from wavering from the grace and truth that there is in Christ– so you can gain mastery and rule over what Christ has called you to rule over, as He has made you Lord over every evil work and by submission to Christ you bring the knees of darkness to the Lordship of Christ [*1 Corinthians 13:11-12; Colossians 2:10; Luke 10:19; Galatians 4:1-2; Hebrews 5:14; Ephesians 4:11-16; 2 Corinthians 10:5*]. I have seen the glory of God. There's yet more deep things to behold. It is as if the ages and generations passed before my eyes, as dust rise with the wind and armies charge before one another in their chariots, and kingdoms rise and fall, of the earth blossoming with flowers and mountains are seen, of fields and peoples, knowing these are all 'happenings' in stages. As if from start to what is to come. It is but a minute scratch of detail of all that there is. Nothing for me to glory in, but the glory of the one who knows all things and control all things. God deserves all glory. These things of the testimonies of the saints written in scriptures are not to hold us in awe of any person, but to yearn for God much deeper in communion and spiritual fellowship. And like Enoch walk with God, and like Adam in the cool of day converse with Him in fellowship. When a spiritual leader talks with God audibly, He is not soliloquising [or as if praying], He is communing with God who is a Spirit being, and can do so in the heart if need be. Christ at the transfiguration spoke with the heavenlies. It takes maturity to operate at this realm. I would also add, maturity involves recognising what love is. This comes with growth, knowledge, time. Often you will have to make decisions– crucial ones, and seemingly flimsy ones, but all impact on your character and ultimately your future. Then it will be important to recognise that love will not mean depriving someone of a good, and comfort, to enrich yourself. To ensure another goes through pain is obviously not a way to preserve a trend. True freedom is loving as Christ loves, and understanding your limitation to determine how another should love– because Christ has already set the standard. We follow God, not culture in our modern day. God's culture never fades. It's loving so we and those around us can gain comfort. Its loving by ensuring others don't suffer so your future can be preserved or made flamboyant– its rather a call to be like Christ. Its loving through the eyes of faith when others don't recognise the human good we do for them, its trusting God preserves our destiny and that though we have been *'engraced'* to be the architect of our times in whatever way, God's blueprint forms our standardisation, as we cannot renegotiate His eternal love, or try to sustain the praise due to His name in our strength– so how are you choosing to love others today? A selfless and mature love, one that is mutually beneficial, sacrificial like Christ's and yet timeless and limitless? Remember, Christ admonishes us to love others as ourselves– not less worthy honour than we would give to the 'me' but perhaps more than you would to yourself to others, but with the great care you would naturally accrue to yourself. To give beyond ourselves is awesome, it is like giving from one's lack or 'deep poverty' as the Churches in Macedonia, as stated in Paul's letter to the Corinthians– now that moves God [*2 Corinthians 8:1-24*]. That takes maturity. This manner of sacrificial living becomes proof of love, ability to lead in maturity, an example for others, a testimony which honours Christ. However, remember the call is to give and love from what He has blessed us with already. This is how revival starts, using your gifts extensively. It is of faith to do this, and even go beyond. God judges us on our abilities, 'talents' he has given, not what we cannot do. If He examines you, perhaps He has given you an ability or priviledge you may have allowed to lie dormant, either through neglect or ignorance. God wants us to find it, use it, and be a blessing by it, as He empowers us. Also recognise this– when as a leader by the timing, benevolence and providence of God, you're able to lead and oversee the affairs of a group of persons equally as gifted as you, even perhaps those who might have a cutting edge over you, wisdom requires that you don't impede their God given abilities, but to ensure they manifest fully and gain whatever they haven't prior and may be entitled to. The reverse is true, where they may be clearly deficient, to train and raise to maturity, so they can be more efficient. And also, to be open to the Spirit's leading where He wants you to step aside, so the more competent can lead. Or can God not bring about this? To the one thinking they're more competent and should lead, remember, God can choose a person you think is not able or qualified to do a magnificent job, so be at peace, and each time be sure to hear God before commenting on who should or who shouldn't. Caleb after the death of Moses approached Joshua, who now led the nation of Israel, and reminded him of the promise made by the Prophet to him and his kindred, when they both undertook an investigation on behalf of their nation– Joshua having the authority showed no restraint but granted it as they were now in the land of promise. That's leadership, keeping a credible promise, dealt by another in leadership prior to you. This manner of attitude or thinking is another example of spiritual maturity, inspire by love. Joshua did not say the promise wasn't made by him, so could not give away the lands to him as territory but was humble to keep the word of his protégé concerning another. That's the grace of mature leadership. How often we hear the stories of some administrators not honouring the commitments to some who may be deserving under their care, and abandoning support for those in need, because of a change of administrative managerial arrangements. Sheer reluctance on this occasion would be shrewdness to cause disadvantage, and unhelpful for their community, as loyalty and progress could have been impeded. I think Joshua showed maturity and grace [see Joshua 14].

xcii.   <u>A new language is only a new way to express the thoughts of your heart, the outflow must remain the same</u>. This is the way we must live as a people that knows God sees the heart, so first our heart must be pure and we must work with the Holy Spirit constantly and progressively to keep it pure, then what flows from it will be pure. Hardly is the outcome pure that comes from a defiled heart, the outlook may seem pure but the definite effect of it will be a tainted form of purity, outward righteousness, pretence, deception. You see it is nothing new for some to keep a sense of approval of love in speech but in the same breath resent, for no cause, or for a cause with no sound or verifiable justification– as complex as that appears. God calls us to resent evil and the proud workers of it, but to love all men, as those who are believers of Christ, and want to see others saved. Spiritual leadership requires not approving of what is done that is not in tandem with the scriptures. For instance, to hate another is wrong, worse still if for no cause– so it matters less how hate is conveyed. If one insults another in Chinese or Greek, or with metaphors, and feel justified because they don't understand proficiently the language, it still would not be polite. Their warm friendship would continue, until they understand. This is different from a situation when fault is overlooked, or when the insulted becomes weary of ignoring– because there is presence of knowledge. The question is not whether one looks good during that time, or whether the friendships endure in the ignorance, but whether to all involved they have a right conscience before God. There is an untapped blessing in living without deception, from a deep place, in our worship of God. We can relate to God from a deep place and place our hearts safely in His hands, because those precious hands have got no spikes– your heart can safely rest in the hands of the saviour's love in the midst of all that's happening [Psalm 42:6-8]. And as we yield to the Spirit we move close to the peace, God has planned for us.

xciii. True leaders encourage, not urge others to take a leap to a defective end. I have seen and observe a few people from a distance who know a particular person may stand no chance at utilising a particular skill but urge them on– almost invisibly mocking, because such a person poses no risk to their own advantage, but where they seemingly do, the same 'encourager' almost completely rescinds from any urges. Incredible– I would say. I have always thought there is a blessing in loving and be loveable, and acting in concert. Some act in this way because they know anyways that so long the mockery is not pointed, they can pitch their tent on both sides of the corner, they can say they encouraged you even though in their hearts they know it amounted to nothing, or they can say it should have amounted to something if the supposed hearer had really taken their advice. How about only encouraging when needed and sincerely? I am sure a person shouldn't feel obligated for a badly turned outcome of an encouragement when given in good faith, except where based on intentional deceit passed on as candid guidance. Consider how important this principle is, and not dismiss this particularly as flimsy– especially as you know that in some jurisdictions certain omission to act could be criminal, as well as false pretence or misrepresentation could present some tortious challenge. Even scripturally we see Christ commend the Samaritan for not omitting to act but that he stopped to give proper assistance. And you now see how grievous it will then be in not only failing to act but actively pointing in a direction that leads to doom. How about hope giving words, words beyond words but true words? Positive action driven words, supporting a people, an idea to fruition, because it advances the kingdom of God's cause, not minding if it limits or expands you personally. The interest and concern at all times is, does a matter truly glorify God. If you realise your words are beginning to muddle up with your genuine intention, then recalibrating your thought and conversation process will be ideal, agreeably this comes with time and much patience and the grace of scripture-based thinking. If what is being done at that time glorifies God, the words should then be– 'How can I genuinely then help this project?' At least if one will not help, don't destroy by passivity or withholding what is due in a situation, or by mobilising others to act against or rejoice in evil. In all things the key is doing what Jesus would do, and we would find that in the word. Whilst on one hand I wholeheartedly urge you to be forthright in your persuasions, I refer you to these scriptures [*Proverbs 9:7-9; Mark 6:11; Genesis 6:3; Ezekiel 3:17-19; Acts 20:26; 1 Kings 22*] to show however that there may be a few times you may have to have restraint and be restive about an obstinate person you are trying to help that will not listen, and stop striving constantly, and just let them go on to be able to tell the difference, this must have been after several warnings– preserving their choice and saving yourself as well from ridicule and unnecessary suffering. I hope this blessed you in your quest for functioning in spiritual leadership.

xciv.   Global influence and salvation– up for it? As you want to be an effective leader that God calls on for global influence, to save a generation from extinction whether morally, or physically or in any good way– then begin to use your positive influence, no matter how little for the force of good. Is God interested in the affairs of men, to guide economic decisions, suggest an ethical blueprint, set a standard for justice that is morally right? Biblical antecedents suggest so [*Genesis 47:13-27; Daniel 4:17; 1 Timothy 2:1-3; 2 Kings 7:1-2; Matthew 5:44-47; 4:8-10*]. I suggest you can do this in partnership with God, and by recognising spiritual hierarchy. I show you a spiritual principle if you can receive and understand it, but yet one which is true– that we all do not have the same pedigree in this world, some are princes or rulers, others are in some other ways credible members of societies, some are employers and others work under the firm, there are the rich and others who may have their needs sufficiently met, or perhaps those who suffer need, there also remains a cross-section of those even with plenty who recognise there are also others who exceed greatly in wealth that dwarfs their advantage, then there is the hierarchy of healthiness as not all are gifted in the same strength. Some desire to go a further distance but discover their body won't do. Age, practice, mental tenacity, maybe genes, all add up to make the realisation that we may be gifted differently. What matters however, is there is an incredible opportunity to access the divine equally and potential to grow. This thought should also inspire our daily relationships in society. Despite the competing complexities of classes in everyday existence spirituality reminds us of that core element of humanity that binds us, which we can explore, and should influence our decision making, to develop affinity for each other as God's unique creature, and seek to even out opportunities, as rarely is anyone sufficient in their self, considering the ever-limiting varied circumstances that may in some occasion impede progress. Only God is unaffected and remains self-sufficient. There is mutual survival and recovery when the power of cooperation and love is harnessed to engineer a better world. In another platform, I would labour more excruciatingly to help you understand this principle even more deeply, but it suffices to say that the imperative on all of goodwill is to seek what makes for peace in a modern global space, and work actively and passively towards making a contribution in achieving this. This is also a form of taking a lead. I call on you take leadership for peace, to adopt spiritual principles, proven, and anchored on Christ a prime example. Aspire for leadership and start developing yourself to not only be served by others but to serve others. Look for credible spaces where monuments for peace can be erected, and trust that the aftermath of your deliberate engagements would create other ends that result in further spirals of peace– that's the dream, that's a worthy goal many who put on this spiritual cloak of leadership have experienced. Christ is the foundation of spiritual leadership, and by considering Him and His thoughts on this matter you will invariably revolutionise your life and those that hear you, for spiritual good– with access to all the blessings in Christ that brings.

Author's Biography Page

Israel Chukwuka Okunwaye, Dip.sc (Benin), LL. B (Benin), BL (Lagos), LLM (Birmingham), M.A (Birmingham)

Israel Chukwuka Okunwaye is a Christian Evangelist and minister of the gospel of Jesus Christ, called of God and with a heart to reach all people with the love that there is in Christ. For many years, now turning into decades he has been communicating this message of the Cross at the grassroots and also on several platforms with the fervour it demands, and with the tremendous spiritual grace the Lord supplies. He has written several works including these books, *Authentic Faith, The Heart of Passion,* and *Rethinking Leadership.* He believes that it is in the loving arms of God you will find all the answers you need. He is the founder of www.glyglobal.com, an online evangelistic network and outreach with free access to credible Christian faith resource and information, which has morphed into an instrumental tool in reaching many with the gospel across the nations, since the first launch many years ago. As a visionary, leader, and anointed speaker, he is graced to teach and minister the word with clarity, and prophetic unction. He also worked briefly as a human rights lawyer in Nigeria and is a staunch advocate for principles of social justice; and is concerned about the plight of the disadvantaged and affirm causes in aid. He believes that the call to Christian living should also drive social action.

He has been priviledged to lead a university campus Christian fellowship with Pentecostal roots, affiliated to Christ's Chosen Church of God Int'l, for some years as President, and thereafter as National President; and was involved in the University of Benin's Christian Community on Campus executive as the Public Relations Officer, a worthy cause of galvanising the body of Christ towards spiritual goals. Prior to this he has been involved with the Scripture Union locally, in encouraging young people and facilitating meetings. In Abuja– Nigeria, he led the work as Evangelism Coordinator under the auspices of the Nigeria Christian Corpers' Fellowship to mobilise efforts at reaching city dwellers and especially those in the rural areas with the gospel, and with practical relief support. Also, working alongside the team at an Elim Pentecostal Church in Selly Oak, Birmingham– UK as Evangelical worker led reaching out to the community and stirred the Church towards soul winning. As one with an evangelistic grace and zeal to see the frontiers for the gospel expand, he has been enabled to serve as Chaplain with CIGB UK [Churches and Industry Group Birmingham and Solihull] with a mission to minister to people at the workplace. He believes in the body of Christ being missional in the community where placed and has organised bible studies to explore and understand the Christian message in response to questions of faith; he continues to be at the forefront of teaching and conveying the word, through his resources, projects, and on speaking platforms. He identifies with the Evangelical Alliance UK as a member.

Evangelist Israel, hold in affirmation the foundational doctrines of faith along with fellow believers, and the Apostles' Creed. He has attended the International Bible Institute of London [IBIOL], Kensington Temple, London, studying the course on Apologetics, and also a Church based ministry training programme, Midlands Ministry Training Course [MMTC], at the Midlands Gospel Partnership, Birmingham.

He is a M.A graduate of the School of Philosophy, Theology and Religion, of University of Birmingham, and has an LLM from the Birmingham Law School. He has also received a BL from the Nigeria Law School, Lagos, after completing his bachelor's degree with the University of Benin.

For further information on ministry update and contact– www.israelokunwaye.com.

www.ingramcontent.com/pod-product-compliance
Lightning Source LLC
Chambersburg PA
CBHW021223090426
42740CB00006B/360